Advance Praise for
End Procrastination Now!

Bill Knaus's comprehensive discussion, based on decades of experience, doesn't just talk about procrastination, it offers structured lessons for assessing and changing patterns of thinking and acting. Easy to read and understand, the book is a valuable resource for becoming more reliable and responsible in everyday life.

—Richard Wessler, Ph.D.
Professor Emeritus, PACE University
Author of *Succeeding with Difficult Clients*

This book sets a new standard for self-help books on how to overcome procrastination. Don't procrastinate. Use the innovative ideas and exercises to stop struggling with procrastination, improve your effectiveness, and raise the quality of your life.

—Arnold A. Lazarus, Ph.D.
Distinguished Professor Emeritus of Psychology,
Rutgers University, ABPP
Coauthor of *The Sixty Minute Shrink*

Anyone struggling with procrastination will find this packed with innovative ideas, quick tips, and powerful self-help exercises to lead a productive and happy life. Read it and profit.

—Janet Wolfe, Ph.D.
Former Executive Director, Albert Ellis Institute
Adjunct Professor, New York University

Internalize this three-pronged approach by the world's foremost authority on the subject and overcome this obstacle to your sustained, future happiness.

—Elliot D. Cohen, Ph.D.
Author of *Critical Thinking Unleashed*

If you are a procrastinator, and a lot of people are, do not delay this time— READ THIS BOOK. *Dr. Knaus is the go-to doc on this serious topic.*

—Frank Farley, Ph.D., L.H.
Professor, Temple University and
Philadelphia Former President,
American Psychological Association

This is a book that should be part-and-parcel of college and university students' required reading lists because it will help them not only to be more successful, but also to enjoy their academic work more, too!

—Rene F.W. Diekstra
Professor of Psychology, Roosevelt Academy,
International Honors College University of Utrecht

End Procrastination Now! *provides a practical and sensible approach to dealing with a habit that can stand in the way of success—in any field. Dr. Bill Knaus's clear writing style and liberal use of examples makes this book a valuable resource for understanding how the pattern of procrastination develops and is maintained. More importantly, this book provides the skills and techniques necessary to take action in making a positive change.*

—Priscilla M. Clarkson
Dean, Commonwealth Honors College,
University of Massachusetts Amherst

Once overcoming denial, the greatest snare for a person trying to overcome an addictive behavior is procrastination. Dr. Knaus has distilled a lifetime of involvement with research and professional experience into a coherent, pragmatic, and cogent program for getting off your butt and just doing it!

—Joe Gerstein, MD, FACP
Founding President, SMART Recovery Self-Help Network

End Procrastination Now!

Get It Done with a
Proven Psychological Approach

William Knaus, Ed.D.

New York   Chicago   San Francisco   Lisbon   London
Madrid   Mexico City   Milan   New Delhi   San Juan
Seoul   Singapore   Sydney   Toronto

1 2 3 4 5 6 7 8 9 0   WFR/WFR   1 5 4 3 2 1 0

ISBN: 978-0-07-166608-4
MHID: 0-07-166608-7

This publication is designed to provide accurate and authoritative information in regard to the subject matter covered. It is sold with the understanding that the publisher is not engaged in rendering legal, accounting, or other professional service. If legal advice or other expert assistance is required, the services of a competent professional person should be sought.

> —*From a declaration of principles jointly adopted by a committee of the American Bar Association and a committee of publishers.*

McGraw-Hill books are available at special quantity discounts to use as premiums and sales promotions, or for use in corporate training programs. To contact a representative please visit the Contact Us pages at www.mhprofessional.com.

Library of Congress Cataloging-in-Publication Data

Knaus, William J.
   End procrastination now! : get it done with a proven psychological approach / by William Knaus.
      p. cm.
   Includes bibliographical references and index.
   ISBN-13: 978-0-07-166608-4 (alk. paper)
   ISBN-10: 0-07-166608-7 (alk. paper)
   1. Procrastination. I. Title.
   BF637.P76K534 2010
   155.2'32—dc22   2009039626

Contents

Foreword

If it weren't for the last minute,
I wouldn't get anything done.

—Anonymous

We all put things off. For example, I managed to put off writing this foreword until the night before the final deadline. Had I read this book sooner, I would have used Bill Knaus's ideas to get the foreword done long before the deadline.

Fortunately, no one procrastinates 100 percent of the time, but everyone procrastinates, some more than others. According to *Psychology Today*, 20 percent of people identify themselves as chronic procrastinators. This book is not focused on procrastinators, but is actually about procrastinating actions, thoughts, and feelings. You'll benefit from this book if you experience occasional procrastinating actions or if you are someone with a more serious problem who has considerable stress and anxiety.

The characteristics commonly associated with procrastination are varied, including low self-confidence, calling attention to how busy you are, stubbornness, manipulation as a means to cope with pressure, and being a frustrated victim. Adlerian psychology has taught me that all behavior has a purpose. So when I read a book on procrastination, I am always looking for the goal or purpose of this type of behavior. Some people use procrastination for the purpose of avoiding difficult or time-consuming tasks. Others use it because they lack knowledge or skills and are afraid that if they screw up, others will find this out (i.e., nothing ventured, nothing lost!). Some use it as a way to express anger (passively) at another by withholding their best efforts. This book will help you learn just how complex human behavior can be and discover the many reasons or goals that might be met by delaying a necessary activity.

Procrastination is often seen as a method for coping with the anxiety involved in making difficult choices or decisions and taking action. This response has become especially prevalent in today's world, where choices are such a big part of everyday life and very few people have been taught choice-making skills. Because we do not know what to do, we do nothing and hope that the situation will go away. This is akin to riding a horse facing backward or swimming upstream. It seldom works, and it can have destructive consequences.

In *End Procrastination Now!* Bill Knaus will teach you a three-pronged approach to cutting through procrastination and accomplishing more in life. The three prongs are:

1. Educate yourself about how procrastination works and change procrastination thinking (the cognitive way).
2. Build tolerance and stamina to tough your way through uncomfortable circumstances (the emotive way).
3. Decide on your direction, behaviorally follow through, and apply what you know to prosper through your work and accomplishments (the behavioral way).

In this book, Bill Knaus demonstrates the rare ability to simplify the complex procrastination process and to provide clear, easy-to-follow steps to learn self-regulation. By following his suggestions, you will learn to be in charge of your life and to restore feelings of strength and purpose. As the Scottish proverb states, "What may be done at any time will be done at no time." Don't put this off! End procrastination now by reading and applying the wisdom in this book.

Jon Carlson, Psy.D., Ed.D., ABPP
Distinguished Professor
Division of Psychology and Counseling
Governors State University

Acknowledgments

I dedicate this book to the memory of Albert Ellis, Ph.D.,
the founder of rational emotive behavioral therapy,
whose tireless work and passionate pursuit of psychological
ways to better people's lives is beyond inspiring.

I'd like to acknowledge the following people for reviewing chapters or contributing ideas to this book: Giulio Bortolozzo; Rina Cohen, Esq.; George Elias, Ed.D.; Edward Garcia, MA; Jon Geis, Ph.D.; Robert Foerster; John Hazen; Nancy Knaus, Ph.D.; Robert Knaus, Ph.D. candidate in mechanical engineering; William Knaus II, MD; Kate Mehuron, Ph.D.; Diane Nadeau; Vince Parr, Ph.D.; Will Ross; Michael Stacey, Ed.D.; Richard Wessler, Ph.D.; and William Wagner.

Albert Ellis Tribute Series Book

End Procrastination Now! is an Albert Ellis Tribute Series Book dedicated to the memory of the famous psychologist and pioneer of rational-emotive-behavioral therapy. The tribute series advisory board members follow:

GENERAL EDITORS: Bill Knaus, Ed.D., Founder of Rational Emotive Education; Former Director of Training, Institute for Advanced Study in Rational Emotive Therapy. Author of seminal work on procrastination. **Jon Carlson**, Psy.D., Ed.D., ABPP Distinguished Professor, Governors State University; Proponent of Adlerian psychotherapy. **Elliot D. Cohen**, Ph.D., Professor, Indian River State College; Adjunct Professor, Florida State University College of Medicine; Founder, Logic-Based Therapy.

TRIBUTE BOOK EDITORIAL ADVISORY BOARD

Irwin Altrows, Ph.D., Associate Fellow and Training Faculty, REBT; Adjunct Assistant Professor (Psychiatry) and Clinical Supervisor (Psychology), Queens University. **Guy Azoula**, Ph.D., French representative for Rational Emotive Education. Supervisor, REBT; Teacher at the French cognitive behavior association. **Aaron T. Beck**, M.D., University Professor of Psychiatry, University of Pennsylvania; President, Beck Institute for Cognitive Therapy and Research. **Judith S. Beck**, Ph.D., Director, Beck Institute for Cognitive Therapy and Research; Clinical Associate Professor of Psychology in Psychiatry, University of Pennsylvania; Founding Fellow and Former President of the Academy of Cognitive Therapy. **Joel Block**, Ph.D., ABPP, Assistant Clinical Professor of Psychiatry, Einstein College of Medicine; Author of books on improving relationships. **Walter Block**, Ph.D., The Harold E. Wirth Eminent Scholar Endowed Chair in Economics at Loyola University; Author of a dozen books and over 200 scholarly articles. **Giulo Bortolozzo**, M.S., Australian representative for Rational Emotive Education; Author of *People and Emotions* and *Have a Go Spaghettio!* **Chuck Carins**, Ph.D., Professor Emeritus, Linguistics, City College, New York. **Nick Cummings**, Ph.D., Former President, American Psychological Association; President, Cummings Foundation. **Rene F.W. Diekstra**, Ph.D., Professor of Psychology, Roosevelt Academy International Honors College, University of Utrecht, The Netherlands. **Rev. Thomas A. Downes**, Ph.D., Long Island College Hospital Chaplain; Master Chaplain, Academy of Certified Chaplains. **Michael R. Edelstein**, Ph.D., Fellow and Supervisor, REBT; Author of *Three-Minute Therapy* and *Stage Fright*; Past President of the Association for Behavioral and Cognitive Therapy. **Debbie Joffe Ellis**, Lic. Psychologist (Australia); Lic. Mental Health Counselor (New York); REBT Fellow, Supervisor, and Presenter; Wife of Albert Ellis. Private practice, New York City. **David Ellis**, JD., Intellectual Property and Patent Attorney; Former Adjunct Professor, University of Florida and Stetson University. **Susan Ellis**, Ph.D., Licensed psychologist; Certified Family Mediator; Author of *Make Sense of Your Dreams* and *Make Sense of Your Feelings*. **Frank Farley**, Ph.D., Former President, American Psychological Association; H. Carnell Professor at Temple University. **Pam Garcey**, Ph.D., Adjunct Psychology Professor, Argosy University-Dallas; Clinical Supervisor, University of Texas Southwestern Medical Center. **Edward Garcia**, MA., Former Director of Training, Institute for Advanced Study in Rational Emotive Therapy; Coauthor of *Building Emotional Muscle* and *Homer the Homely Hound Dog*. **H. Jon Geis**, Ph.D., Original Director of Training, Institute for Advanced Study in Rational Emotive Therapy; Taught at New York University, Columbia University, and Yeshiva University. **Joe Gerstein**, MD., Founding President, SMART Recovery Self-Help Network; Harvard Medical School (retired). **Russ Greiger**, Ph.D., REBT Supervisor; Adjunct Professor at the University of Virginia; Six books and over 50 professional papers and chapters on REBT. **Nancy Haberstroh**, MBA, Ph.D., Primary U.S. representative of Rational Emotive Education; Director of Psychological Services, Monson Developmental Center. **Steven C. Hayes**, Ph.D., Foundation Professor of Psychology, University of Nevada, Reno. **Howard Kassinove**, Ph.D., ABPP, Professor of Psychology and Director, Institute for the Study and Treatment of Anger and Aggression at Hofstra University. **Tony Kidman**, Ph.D., Director of the Health Psychology Unit, University of Technology, Sydney, Australia. Member of the Order of Australia. **Sam Klarreich**, Ph.D., President, The Berkeley Centre for Effectiveness, Toronto, Canada. **Gerald Koocher**, Ph.D., ABPP, Former President, American Psychological Association; Dean and Professor, School of Health and Sciences, Simmons College. **Paul Kurtz**, Ph.D., Professor Emeritus, Philosophy, State University of New York at Buffalo; Founding President, Center for Inquiry; Author of 50 books. **Arnie Lazarus**, Ph.D., ABPP, Professor Emeritus, Rutgers University; Founder, Multimodal Psychotherapy. **Barry Lubetkin**, Ph.D., Founding Copresident Behavioral Therapy Center, New York;

Author of books on resolving marital and social anxieties. **John Minor**, Ph.D., Associate Fellow and training faculty, REBT; Adjunct Professor, University of California. **John C. Norcross**, Ph.D., Professor of Psychology & Distinguished University Fellow, University of Scranton. **Christine A. Padesky**, Ph.D.,Distinguished Founding Fellow, Academy of Cognitive Therapy; Cofounder, Center for Cognitive Therapy; Author of best-selling *Mind Over Mood*. **Vince Parr**, Ph.D., President, Rational Living Foundation, Tampa, FL. **Leon Pomeroy**, Ph.D., Adjunct Faculty, George Mason University; President of The Robert S. Hartman Institute; Author of *The New Science of Axiological Psychology*. **Aldo R. Pucci**, Psy.D., President, National Association of Cognitive-Behavioral Therapists. **Roberta Richardson**, Ph.D., Vice-Chair of Association of REBT, U.K. **Will Ross**, Webmaster, REBTnetwork.org; Long-term voluntary practice in the application of REBT on suicide prevention hotlines. **Gayle Rosellini**, MS., Specialist in 501-c-3, private, nonprofit agencies; Treatment of addictions and criminality; Author "Of Course You're Angry." **Nosheen Kahn Rahman**, Ph.D., Professor/Director of Centre for Clinical Psychology, University of the Punjab, Lahore, Pakistan. **Richard S. Schneiman**, Ph.D., Codirector Intermountain Center for REBT, Salt Lake City, Utah. **Sanjay Singh**, MD, DNB, Ph.D., REBT and REE Representative in India; Associate Professor, Department of Dermatology, Institute of Medical Sciences, Banaras Hindu University, Varanasi, India. **Deborah Steinberg**, MSW, Fellow and Supervisor, REBT; Child specialty: character development and moral education; Author of *How to Stick with a Diet*. **Thomas Szasz**, M.D., Professor of Psychiatry Emeritus, SUNY Upstate Medical University, Syracuse, New York. **Danny Wedding**, Ph.D., MPH, Professor of Psychiatry, University of Missouri-Columbia; Director, Missouri Institute of Mental Health. **Richard Wessler**, Ph.D., Former Director of Training, Institute for Advanced Study of Rational Emotive Therapy; Professor Emeritus, Pace University; Cofounder, Cognitive Appraisal Therapy. **Janet L. Wolfe**, Ph.D., Former Executive Director, Albert Ellis Institute; Adjunct Professor, New York University; Private practice, New York City.

Introduction

End Procrastination with a Three-Step Approach

D o you want to accomplish more in life? Do your procrastination habits get in the way of your doing so? If your answer to these questions is yes, in *End Procrastination Now!* you'll learn how to take charge of your life as you watch procrastination fade in your rearview mirror.

If you want to end your membership in the procrastinator's club, what are you up against? Procrastination is among the most pervasive, tenacious, and complex of personal challenges. For many, it's a conundrum. Like other problem habits, however, it has vulnerabilities. You'll learn to exploit those vulnerabilities by using powerful awareness and action approaches in which you work against procrastination from the inside out.

If you want to cut through procrastination, you've already started—you are reading this book. The next step is to employ the unique three-pronged approach that I'll show you here, use these ideas, and apply the exercises to the challenge of breaking free from procrastination.

In *End Procrastination Now!*, I'll be with you all the way to share ideas about how to follow through on what you believe is important to do. You'll learn how to end procrastination by following a *do-it-now* path. On this path, you do reasonable things in a reasonable way within a reasonable time to improve your health, happiness, and a deserved sense of accomplishment. But first, let's go over some general concepts about procrastination. This information will put in context some of the things that I'll be discussing in the chapters ahead.

What Is Procrastination?

Did you know that the Latin origin of the word *procrastination* is *pro* (forward) plus *crastinus* (belonging to tomorrow)? However, procrastination is much more than postponing something, and the concept isn't as simple as many people think. Here's my definition: *procrastination is an automatic problem habit of putting off an important and timely activity until another time. It's a process that has probable consequences.*

This common human condition involves a negative perception about an anticipated activity, always involves an urge to diverge by substituting something less relevant, and is practically always accompanied by procrastination thinking, such as, "I'll do this later when I feel ready." More than a simple act of avoidance, procrastination involves a process of interconnected perceptions and thoughts (the cognitive component), emotions and sensations (the emotive component), and actions (the behavioral component). Procrastination is far more complex than a simple behavioral problem.

From a minor "later is better" procrastination seed can grow a bigger problem habit. A procrastination decision to delay brings immediate relief and hope. These feelings of relief and hope reinforce the procrastination decision, making other procrastination decisions more likely in the future. Following that, you can make excuses to justify the delay or ask for an extension for yet another day. Procrastination can include intricate patterns of delay.

Let's look at an example: Jane's struggle with procrastination over a written analysis of her organization's quarterly financial results. After weeks of delay, Jane decided to finish the report over the weekend. After Sunday lunch, she was ready to start, and she walked sluggishly to her computer, wincing at the thought of writing. The following sequence of events occurred:

1. As Jane sat down to get started on her report, she heard the call of her lawn's long grass, which needed mowing.
2. Jane walked toward the mower, pulled the cord, and heard it come to life.
3. She felt relief as she thought she'd get the report done after raking the grass clippings. By concentrating on the mowing, she put aside the nagging reminder in the back of her mind that she felt in her gut.
4. As she finished mowing, Jane noticed her neighbor sipping lemonade by her pool and walked over to chitchat.
5. After catching up on things with her neighbor, Jane returned home to cook dinner.
6. After a filling meal, she went to take a nap. She said to herself, "I'll start later, when I feel alert."
7. Waking up from her nap, Jane realized that it was time for the nightly news. She told herself that after the news, she'd stay up late and get the report done.
8. The news ended, and Jane returned to the computer. However, her fingers had a life of their own. She clicked the solitaire icon and felt jived about the game.
9. Before she realized it, it was midnight. She thought, "It is too late to start now. I'll start early in the morning." She felt good about her new resolve
10. Her alarm rang at 7:00 a.m. Now panicked to get ready for work, Jane had no time to start the report.

11. Arriving at work, she decided to get the busywork out of the
    way. By the time she finished her phone calls and e-mails, it
    was time for lunch.
12. Jane skipped lunch, rushed to meet the 4:00 deadline, and
    ran out of time.
13. Frazzled, she asked her boss for an extension because of
    "complications" and got an extra day.
14. She blocked out everything else and finished.
15. Annoyed, Jane blamed herself, thinking that she could have
    done better had she started earlier, and swore, "I'll start
    earlier next time."
16. With the next report, she repeated a similar pattern.

Jane's style of procrastinating suggests that procrastination
can be both automatic and extensive. (We'll revisit Jane's procrastination problem habit in later chapters, where I'll show you how
Jane used a basic cognitive, emotive, and behavioral approach to
prevent procrastination.)

Who Procrastinates?

Procrastination is an equal opportunity habit that interferes with
the productivity of people from every economic level, profession,
age, or other demographic category. Practically everyone has at
least one (and probably more) serious procrastination challenge
to meet, especially workplace procrastination. A 2007 salary.com
survey suggests that U.S. workers, on average, waste 20 percent
of the workday. Procrastination researchers Joseph Ferrari and his
colleagues surveyed white- and blue-collar workers living in such
diverse countries as the United States, England, Australia, Turkey,
Peru, Spain, and Venezuela. They found that about 25 percent
persistently hinder themselves through workplace procrastination.
Does this mean that the others are relatively procrastination-free?
Hardly! Few, if any, workers are procrastination-free.

Different people procrastinate for different reasons and in different ways. Some postpone decisions where there is no guarantee for success; others find creative ways to delay and put off unpleasant tasks. Persistent forms of procrastination are serious problems for hundreds of millions of people, especially for those who tie their self-worth to their performance and whose procrastination may also contribute to stress-related health problems.

I don't know anyone who chooses to develop a procrastination habit. This would be like choosing depression over emotional health. Choice comes into play when you recognize that you can either take corrective action or do nothing and hope for the best. Choose to change, and it is your responsibility to take corrective action. However, change is also a process, not an event, and I'll tell you more about that in Chapter 1.

Changing the Procrastination Habit

If procrastination is an automatic habit, are you stuck? Fortunately, you have alternative choices that you can employ against procrastination. Changing erroneous thinking (the cognitive way), developing tolerance for discomfort (the emotive way), and graduated exposure (the behavioral way) can disable procrastination and prevent recurrences.

In "The Road Not Taken," the American poet Robert Frost showed the inevitability of choice. He wrote the poem to describe the dilemma of a friend who, after choosing one path, would fret because he had not traveled the other. Frost's poem knocks at the door of human inquisitiveness, and its last verse is among the most frequently quoted: "Two roads diverged in a wood, and I— I took the one less traveled by, And that has made all the difference." Here we see an interesting example of how we can view the automatic habit of procrastination as being tempered by the idea of choice.

The father of American psychology, William James, got an important insight into the importance of choice. You see, James suffered from recurring depression. After trying the behavioral methods of his day, James found no relief. He needed a new option. He found it in the free-will philosophy of the nineteenth-century French philosopher Charles Renouvier: this is the idea that you can choose one way when you could have chosen another. James decided that he could try other ways. For example, he believed that by changing his thinking, he could change his life.

Another view of freedom of choice is that of doing as you please. But might this be the path to self-indulgence? Consider an alternative view. Some of our most impressive accomplishments involve hardships. Have you ever done something of significance that did not have a cost?

What can be said about following the path on which procrastination casts its shadow? The experiences will be different from those found on a path of productive accomplishments. The procrastination path is often worn, and the one of purposeful, productive, and creative efforts and products covers exciting new ground. On this path, commitment and persistence count more than undisciplined ability. However, those with high ability who impose restrictions on themselves to support persistence with productive actions can justifiably be counted among the top performers.

Lose the "I'm a Procrastinator" Label

Before we move ahead to discuss the cognitive, emotive, and behavioral approach to kicking the procrastination habit, there are a few additional foundation concepts to cover. As a practical matter, people may loosely say, "I'm a procrastinator." Upon reflection, few of them could legitimately say that they were only one way or another; thus, negative generalizations about yourself are false depictions. If you are only a procrastinator, how do you change who you are?

Procrastination is not a black-and-white issue where you either are a procrastinator or you are not. You can procrastinate in some areas of your life and still have many admirable qualities and accomplishments. Instead, procrastination represents a changeable process. Thus, it is infinitely more reasonable and realistic to think about changing your actions or habits than to pigeonhole yourself.

Remember that words have the power to color perspective. Think of the words *loser* and *winner*. Do they create different images? If you label yourself a loser, how will you feel and what will you do? Character generalizations like "loser" or "winner" suffer from the same flaw as the label "procrastinator."

Labeling yourself a procrastinator is a choice, but one that you'll have trouble justifying. Procrastination is relative. No one I know procrastinates 100 percent of the time, and no one is 100 percent efficient or effective. You might more accurately describe yourself as a person who procrastinates in specific ways, but who is timely and effective in other ways.

You may not like your procrastinating behavior. You may change what you don't like. But procrastination does not define you as a whole.

If you call yourself a procrastinator, this may have no more general meaning than descriptively calling yourself an engineer or middle-aged. You know you're a pluralistic person with thousands of attributes who plays dozens of roles in life. But here's the problem: most people think categorically and not pluralistically. Thus, you risk identifying with the label in a way that suggests that you have no choice but to imitate the label.

Overcome the Fear of Failure in Order to Curb Procrastination

Procrastination has many causes, such as tension avoidance. If you don't like a pressing project, you put it on the back burner.

Among other causes, anxiety can ignite procrastination. When you are anxious, you look to the future with apprehension. A threat is coming. You believe that you can't control the situation. You have an urge to diverge to a safer activity. "Fear of failure" is commonly used to describe this procrastination process. However, "failure anxiety" is a better phrase.

Perfectionism can provoke anxious thinking and spur procrastination. You may act as if you believe that you are either a success or a failure based on your ability to meet high performance expectations. If you don't think that you have the resources to meet your lofty standards, this belief can kick procrastination into gear. However, you can help yourself dump this self-sabotage by eliminating the idea of failure.

Beyond taxes and death, there are few guarantees in life. Failure, or falling short of your standards for success, is another guaranteed area. This will, from time to time, happen. It's how you deal with the inevitable setbacks and failures in life that makes the difference.

A no-failure philosophy can make a difference if it helps free you from inhibitions and fears about undertaking something new, difficult, or complicated that you might normally put off. Before looking at the idea behind a nonfailure philosophy, let's look at some ideas about failure:

- Failure is like a passing breeze among everything else that is part of nature. It is a normal part of living and learning. You don't make a sale every time you try. You may take a bar examination more than once. You have no luck as a professional Bigfoot investigator. During a recessionary period, your stock portfolio gets hit.
- Some failures have consequences. The person who wishes to get drunk without ill effects is living in a dream world. In the world of commerce, failing to produce is likely to result in someone else getting your job.

- Most failures are fictional, such as thinking that if you are not 100 percent perfect in whatever you undertake, you are a failure. That show-stopping idea can lead to many manufactured miseries. Who's perfect?
- Failure can be instructive when you use its consequences for self-correction. Sometimes the instruction is painful. Sometimes the consequences lead to new insights and discoveries.

The fear of failure trap has different window views. The irrational perfectionism view is through a watermarked prism window. The prism distorts what you experience. The watermarks represent a contingent worth point of view: you're noble if your life is filled with successes; your failures define you. This black-white perspective is a slippery slope toward procrastination.

Can you spring free from this success-failure trap? Fear of failure is a fictional trap that has everything to do with you, and little to do with what you do. If there is no failure, you have nothing to fear. Fortunately, you can eliminate failure. Well, at least in the area of your self-development.

View your self-development efforts as experiments and your plans as hypotheses. That changes the view. Now you are operating like a scientist. You test the plan and judge the result, not yourself. If you don't like the result, you adjust and retest the plan.

Introducing this new tolerance-building line of thought into a well-practiced contingency worth script is not an overnight deal. New philosophies take time to take hold.

Take on the Do-It-Now Philosophy

The *do-it-now* philosophy is to do reasonable things in a reasonable way within a reasonable time to increase your chances for health, happiness, and desired accomplishments. Following the do-it-now way, you simultaneously attack procrastination and responsibly follow through on what is important to do. You contest your urges to diverge by refusing to distract yourself as you work hard at what you may be tempted to put off. How you go about executing this *dual-change* challenge makes the difference. It's here that knowledge and know-how count. You develop this ability by combining the processes that you find work best for you and by repeating the application until you overlearn it.

You're starting from a positive point. You already have the means to take charge of what you think, feel, and do to meet the challenge. Your challenge is to unleash yourself to do what you can accomplish.

The do-it-now philosophy highlights a path to progressive mastery over procrastination. By following this philosophy, you act to break a procrastination habit. In executing this lifestyle shift, you recognize sidetracking self-statements, perceived emotional threats, and diversionary activities that all hinder productive results.

The do-it-now process won't take hold overnight. It takes time and practice to successfully contest old procrastination habits and build positive follow-through ones, but with this positive attitude, in conjunction with the cognitive, emotive, and behavioral approach that I'll show you, you'll be on the road to overcoming procrastination.

End Procrastination with the Cognitive, Emotive, and Behavioral Approach

By changing negative thinking, defusing stress emotions, and engaging in proactive behaviors, you can change your life for the better. I'll tell you how.

The cognitive, behavioral, and emotive skills that you can learn are durable and are especially useful in making and sustaining lifestyle changes that most people put off, such as such as weight control, exercise, and stress reduction.

You can learn and apply the methods with confidence. Cognitive behavioral therapy is an evidence-based system that is supported by more than 400 random control studies. The system is also supported by 16 meta-analyses A meta-analysis is a study of studies that uses a statistical synthesis of the research data. The cognitive behavioral approach is the dominant system because it's probably the most effective way to make and maintain important cognitive, emotive, and behavioral changes.

Evidence-based cognitive, emotive, and behavioral methods can be self-taught. The most highly rated self-help books are those that focus on a specific theme, apply empirically grounded cognitive behavioral methods, and are written by doctoral-level mental health professionals who are trained in the methods. This book meets those criteria.

This is not a work harder and work longer type of book. Sure, there are times when maximum efforts are important. However, most of life involves typical performance, which is what you do on a day-to-day basis. The idea is to end procrastination interferences so that you can prosper without the pain that commonly accompanies needless self-imposed delays. You can then make that maximum effort sooner when it is necessary. You'll have more time for fun and for higher levels of accomplishment when you gain time normally lost through procrastination.

In *End Procrastination Now!* you'll learn a three-pronged approach to cut through procrastination and accomplish more of what you want during the time you'd ordinarily procrastinate. This program also applies to meeting deadlines and due dates without the usual last-minute rush. The three prongs are:

- Educate yourself about how procrastination works and how to change procrastination thinking (the cognitive way).
- Build tolerance and stamina to tough your way through uncomfortable circumstances (the emotive way).
- Decide your direction, behaviorally follow though, and apply what you know to prosper through your work and your accomplishments (the behavioral way).

This three-pronged program applies to reducing negatives (procrastination) and advancing your positive choices and purposes. Indeed, reducing a needless negative (procrastination) is also very positive.

The three prongs are separate but unified. Making positive changes in one area can have a beneficial effect on the others.

The cognitive, emotive, and behavioral approaches apply to broad challenges, such as how to make real personal changes that stick. For example, in the process of curbing procrastination, you'll learn how to meet challenges decisively and free yourself from stresses that contribute to procrastination and that result from procrastination.

The Cognitive Approach

The cognitive approach is grounded in thinking about your thinking and acting to change automatic negative thoughts (ANT) that lead to unpleasant emotions and self-defeating behaviors. A big part of the challenge is knowing when and how to recognize that thinking, and how to use this knowledge to prevent or short-circuit procrastination.

You can teach yourself to dispute procrastination thinking. You'll find guidelines, tips, and methods for doing so throughout the book. Procrastination thinking, such as, "I'll get to this later," represents specious reasoning that you can quickly learn to debunk. You may fear failure because you fear that rejection will follow. You put off actions in the service of avoiding what is often a fictional fear. Part 1 of *End Procrastination Now!* will show you how to recognize and deal with these cognitive barriers.

The Emotive Approach

Prior to procrastinating, you're likely to experience some form of unpleasant emotion(s) about starting an activity. You may feel tempted to duck the tension and follow the path of least resistance by substituting an emotionally safe diversionary activity for the one you feel uncomfortable doing. However, the delayed task normally doesn't disappear, and the unpleasant feeling is likely to remain despite your best discomfort-dodging efforts.

Procrastination may start as an emotional reaction to a complex task, an activity with a reward that appears too far in the future, or something that you view as frustrating, unpleasant, or threatening. The task may evoke anxiety. It may be a default reaction to a whisper of negative emotion.

You may set emotional conditions for action. You may think that you need to feel inspired before you can act. If you wait to feel inspired, you may join the characters in Samuel Beckett's play *Waiting for Godot*. (Godot is a no-show.) However, when it comes to following through on unpleasant but necessary responsibilities, it is wise to lead with your intellect and force yourself to get past emotional barriers and onto a productive path. You'll learn many powerful techniques in Part 2 to help you handle emotional barriers to success and happiness effectively.

The Behavioral Approach

When you procrastinate, you practically always substitute something less pressing or important for the activity that you delay. You may do a less pressing but more important activity. However, most behavioral diversions tend to be bottom-drawer-type activities, such as reading the comic section of your newspaper instead of digesting a complex new government regulation that will cause an important change in the way you do business.

In Part 3, you'll find a wealth of behavioral prescriptions to curb behavioral diversions and spur productive efforts.

A combination of procrastination thinking, emoting, and behavioral habits can overwhelm even an initial affirmative choice to stop procrastinating. A transition from procrastination to a productive follow-through habit takes time and practice, using the powerful cognitive, emotive, and behavioral antidotes that you'll find in this book. However, this program has a large value-added feature. You can apply this comprehensive psychology self-help program again and again to get more of what you want and deserve out of life. Try it and see!

By developing your positive cognitive, emotive, and behavioral skills, you can quickly put yourself on the path to self-efficacy. The belief that you have the ability to organize, regulate, and direct your actions toward positive goals is among the most studied in psychology and is associated with higher levels of productive performance. Low self-efficacy, procrastination, and substandard performances are understandably associated.

By taking a cognitive, emotive, and behavioral approach, you can extend and refine your productive skills. However, this is not done in a vacuum: you engage in purposeful projects that yield meaningful results. Another element is accepting that major, purposeful life goals are accomplished small step by small step. Keep your eye on the prize of accomplishing more by procrastinating less and keep moving toward this objective.

In addition to tactics and strategies for ending procrastination, you'll find references to the scientific literature on procrastination. Some of this work is promising, such as recent research that deals with a segment of a theory on procrastination that I outlined. However, much of the research on procrastination suffers from a constant error. The student surveys conducted by the majority of social scientists represent a very limited sample in the broader social context of different peoples and groups. In drawing attention to a specific characteristic, such as procrastination, this can lead to a focusing illusion that can be a significant source of error. These consistent errors are scattered about in University of Calgary Professor Piers Steel's summary of the procrastination research. Perhaps in the next decade we'll find a rising tide of outcome research concerning what people can actually do to kick the procrastination habit. Until then, the three-pronged approach is based on strong findings from clinical research in the area of taking corrective actions. What we already know about curbing procrastination can only get better.

End Procrastination Now! Your Plan

Throughout this book, you'll find dozens of coordinated ways to advance your productive interests and decrease procrastination interferences. As an additional tool, at the end of each chapter of *End Procrastinating Now!* you'll find space for a procrastination journal of what you found important to remember, what you planned to do, what you did to execute the plan, what resulted, and what you can do with what you learned. This journal will give you an ongoing record that you can refer to whenever you want to review what you accomplished and use what you learned to move yourself to a higher level of confidence and accomplishment. It consists of four parts: key ideas, action plan, implementing actions, and what you learned. You can refer to the information when you want to remind yourself of what works for you, or use it as a tool to build your own program by putting together your own action plans.

There is much that you can do to gain relief from procrastination. By taking a longer-term self-education perspective, you are less likely to follow the procrastination path. By looking for opportunities to pit reason against procrastination deceptions, you are less likely to skid onto the procrastination path. By accepting unpleasant emotions and sensations as temporary, you are less likely to recoil from normal forms of discomfort. By forcing yourself to start taking corrective actions, you load the dice in favor of less hassle, more accomplishments, and a healthier and happier lifestyle. Let's get started!

PART ONE

The Cognitive Approach: Change Procrastination Thinking through Self-Awareness

1

Perspectives on Procrastination and Awareness for Change

Procrastination can be puzzling. This variable and complex process comes with lists of causes, symptoms, jokes, and horror stories. It can range from sporadic to persistent. It can be obvious or arrive in disguise. In this chapter, you'll begin to see procrastination from different angles and learn to adjust your level of aspiration concerning the time and resources you will need if you are to take corrective action against procrastination.

It's important to recognize that awareness is the very first step in identifying procrastination traps in order to make positive changes that can overcome the procrastination habit. However, as Alfred Korzybski, founder of General Semantics (an educational discipline on the accurate use of words), said, "The map is not the same as the territory. It's a symbol and guide. You learn the territory by engaging the process." So let's get started!

General Procrastination Styles

Procrastination is a needless delay of a timely and relevant activity. This definition applies across situations ranging from returning a phone call to creating a business plan to quitting smoking.

Occasional procrastination delays in areas of your life that are of relatively low importance are not the end of the world. If you normally shop for groceries once a week and you put off shopping for a day, this procrastination act is inconsequential. However, persistently putting off a number of minor and middle-valued activities is self-defeating if you routinely feel swamped by things you delayed yesterday.

Regardless of whether your procrastination is erratic or persistent, taking action to stop procrastination habits or patterns can lift artificial limits that you previously placed on your life. Any area of procrastination is grist for the mill for purposes of teaching yourself to rid yourself of the procrastination act on the way to disabling the pattern. This is a radically different way of thinking from that of time management hawks, whose views are calculated to get people to work harder and to put out more under umbrella terms of working smarter and easier.

Some causes of procrastination are social, some are linked to brain processes, and others are belief-driven or reliant on temperament and mood. Some forms of procrastination can also be connected to anxiety—feeling uncomfortable about being judged or evaluated. Combinations of motives for procrastination tend to vary in each individual situation. However, it is both the consistency of the procrastination process and the great diversity in situations that set procrastination apart from conditions. A cued panic reaction normally takes far less time and effort to change than a broad pattern of procrastination that may show up in different venues and in surprising and unexpected ways. Let's take a look at general forms of procrastination.

Deadline Procrastination

Deadlines have an endpoint and are partially connected to some sort of rule or regulation that you often can't control but that requires your compliance. When you think of procrastination, you may think of missing deadlines or rushing to meet them. That's a common view of procrastination. Not surprisingly, deadline procrastination is the act of waiting as long as possible before taking action to meet a deadline.

Work life is ruled by timelines, processes, and deadlines. Let's say you are working on your company's semiannual advertising brochure. To get it out at the appointed time, you'll need to take certain steps, such as preparing the content and design, getting it printed, and getting it distributed, in accordance with a schedule. If these activities were not regulated, the advertising brochure might be completed in a disorganized manner.

When a timeline and instructions are fuzzy, but the deadline is clear, you have a special challenge. You may see tasks with vague instructions as something to do later. When a task's purpose and instructions are clear and concrete (when, where, and how), you are more likely to do it. Thus, if you are not sure, ask. And if there is no clear structure, invent one!

You may have a deadline for a long and complex project, and the only reward in sight is the relief you expect to feel when it's done. In this case, you may face another set of challenges that has to do with the distance from your internal reward system. Pigeons will work for small immediate rewards but slack off for a larger reward that requires more work. Monkeys will get distracted and procrastinate when the reward is too far in the distance. We're not far from our mammalian roots when it comes to putting something off when the reward is distant and requires a lot of work. Humans will tend to go for quick rewards and discount bigger future rewards. We'll tend to delay starting projects that appear complex or ambiguous, or that promote uncertainty. Conflicts between our primitive impulses to avoid discomfort over complexity and our higher cognitive functions to solve problems can interfere with rational decision making and promote delays. Thus, a complex long-term project may be like the perfect storm unless you do something else first.

Deadline situations are often trade-off situations. If you want to get a paycheck, you follow the organization's processes and schedule and avoid procrastinating. The organization gets what it wants, which is a work product, and you get what you want, which is payment for your services. When you have a deadline in the future and the project is complex and requires consistent work, you may have no alternative other than to start early and invest significant time and effort in the process. If the process is internally rewarding, then that may suffice. Otherwise, you'd wisely set periodic rewards following intermediate deadlines that you set for yourself following the completion of predefined chunks of work.

If procrastination interferes with a productive long-term work process, a chart reminder may help you keep perspective on the purpose, deadline, timeline, and procrastination risk factor:

What is the purpose?	What is the deadline?	What is the timeline for the critical phases of the project?	Where is procrastination likely to interfere in the process?

Remember, being aware and cognizant of your procrastination habit is the first step in our three-pronged cognitive, emotive, and behavioral approach to defeat procrastination. Reminders can be helpful. Human memory is fallible. Some delays are due to forgetfulness. You can meet some deadlines automatically with mechanical processes, like automatic payments to utility companies and mortgage holders, that eliminate work. This is also an efficient thing to do. You can use tickler files, calendar notations, iPhones, PDAs, and your cell phone to remind you of important dates.

Personal Procrastination

Deadline procrastination is just the tip of the procrastination iceberg. A bigger and more serious challenge may involve personal procrastination. Personal procrastination is habitually putting off personally relevant activities, such as facing a needless inhibiting fear. You stick with a stressful job that you want to ditch. You feel timid, and you promise yourself that you'll take an assertiveness class someday. Instead of engaging in self-improvement activities, you watch TV and read tabloid magazines.

Because self-development activities are just about you, and because they are open-ended with an indefinite start date, this may not seem like procrastination. However, it meets the definition. The following chart is a classic framework for identifying your top self-development priority. The process involves defining your most pressing and important self-development goal or priority and other activities that are worth pursuing. Engaging in activities that are not important and nonpressing before all the activities above them are done may waste your time and resources. If you emphasize not important and nonpressing activities over your number one priority, you're procrastinating by using the bottom-drawer activities as diversions. For example, if you face a health risk and you read Hollywood scandal magazines in lieu of taking steps to stop smoking, you need to think about what you're doing. The following chart is an example.

ACTION	Important	Useful	Not Important
Pressing	Quitting smoking to reduce high risk for emphysema and cancer.	Dealing with snake phobia, as garter snake spotted in park.	Neighbor pushing you to join local poker club for social purposes. Nice to do, but far from top of list.
Nonpressing	Dealing with fear of flying. No trips currently planned that require flying.	Organize computer files to access related data.	Keeping up with news about Hollywood scandals

Now it's your turn to define what are the most pressing and important things for you to do.

ACTION	Important	Useful	Not Important
Pressing			
Nonpressing			

Omissions. What you omit doing may be a prime area of personal procrastination. Dick was retired and spent a great deal of his time complaining. He complained about his woman friend and how her ongoing misery and physical complaints affected his mood. He complained about his breakfast group, whom he saw as the cold blanket squad who complained about their aches and pains and the importance of maintaining the status quo. He complained about lost opportunities and the hassles of life. What did these complaints have in common? They were all diversions.

Dick's pressing and important and nonpressing and not important self-development chart helped him isolate several areas of procrastination. First and foremost, he wanted to learn how to do teleconferencing on his computer so that he could keep in direct contact with his children and grandchildren. He wanted to visit art centers, travel, and study politics. His complaints covered up what he did with his time, which was mostly sleeping during the daytime and watching television at night. Once we established his priorities and identified the futility of complaining, then Dick started to work on his personal development challenges, which were no longer mysterious.

Simple Procrastination

Simple procrastination is a default procrastination style in which you resist and recoil from any uncomplicated activity that you find mildly inconvenient or unpleasant. This may start with a momentary hesitation that, unless it is quickly overridden by a productive action, may trigger a procrastination default reaction. This hesitation process may have to do with the way the brain works.

The brain may be wired to promote a *later* factor, or an automatic slowing in decision making: the time it takes the brain to voluntarily react to a sensory signal is longer than expected. This may be a result of decision-making and delay issues caused by your higher mental processes having difficulty understanding the signals from lower brain functions. The potential conflict between lower brain processes and cognitive decision-making processes may partially explain how a simple procrastination default reaction starts. If you have a discomfort sensitivity triggered by this conflict, and then you extend the delay to the level of procrastination, the *later* factor suggests a possible mechanism. But whether this is the real mechanism or the reaction is caused by something else, the solution remains the same. You have to act to override this biological resistance.

Complex Procrastination

When procrastination includes coexisting conditions, it's complex. Complex procrastination is the kind of procrastination that is accompanied by other factors, such as self-doubts or perfectionism. Complex procrastination is a laminated variety. You can separate the layers and address each as a subissue. However, the layers tend to be interconnected, so by addressing one layer, you may weaken the connection with the others. For example, let's say you have an urge to engage in diversionary activities. You switch to doing something trivial, perhaps something more costly. You need to pay a bill, but instead, you go to a casino to gamble. You then try to forget your new gambling debts by turning on the TV.

When you face and overcome coexisting conditions, your goal of cutting back on procrastination doesn't go away. You may have eliminated one of the complex layers; however, procrastination often has a life of its own and goes on as it did before. You still have to deal with your procrastination habit if you want to free yourself from this burden by changing procrastination thinking, developing emotional tolerance, and behaviorally pursuing productive goals.

Symptoms, Defenses, Resistances, and Problem Habits

Procrastination can be a symptom, a defense, a problem habit, or a combination of these general conditions. It can be a *symptom* of a complex form of procrastination, such as worrying about worry and then putting off learning cognitive coping skills to defuse the worry. Busywork can be a symptom of underlying tension for a problem that you want to avoid. This busyness is a kind of behavioral diversion, which is as productive as racing down a dead-end street.

A procrastination symptom can be especially helpful when it provides cues about an omission that needs recognizing and correcting. For example, the English naturalist Charles Darwin put off his medical studies and eventually came up with a theory of evolution by following his real passion. His *symptom* was his distraction from his medical school studies. Let's say your family persuades you to run the family sporting goods store. You have limited interest in managing the store, but you do so out of duty. Procrastination surfaces when it comes time to order new goods, keep up with paperwork, and deal with personnel matters, but you are quick and efficient in making better use of existing shelf space, creating an attractive façade, and landscaping, because what you really want to do is study architecture. What you emphasize in your work is a testament to your personal interest.

Procrastination can be a *defense* against conditions, such as fear of failure, failure anxiety, and fear of blame. If you tend to think in a perfectionistic way and you believe that you cannot succeed at the level at which you think that you should, this may trigger procrastination by causing you to exert only halfhearted efforts or to decide to do something else altogether. If you focus on the horrors of failure, you may omit looking at a probable mechanism, such as perfectionist beliefs. Fear of success is another form of failure anxiety that can have the same impact as fear of failure. You believe that if you succeed, the pressure for you to do more will increase. In this frame of mind, it is easier to delay now than to risk failure later. You have other ways to construe these possibilities. Putting off thinking about these evaluative fears, and taking possible countermeasures, is a form of *conceptual procrastination*.

You can gain control over the causes of procrastination by addressing them. However, an automatic procrastination habit may remain, and you may continue to have an automatic urge to procrastinate.

Habits, even procrastination habits, may operate blindly when they serve no useful purpose. To respond to an automatic procrastination habit, plan on overpracticing your counter-procrastination strategy to weaken the strength of this automatic habit.

Procrastination is normally a complex problem process. Separating procrastination into the three categories of symptom, defense, and problem habit gives you a way to frame what is going on when you procrastinate. A good assessment for complex procrastination can point to change techniques that you may find useful. When you target potential underlying mechanisms for procrastination, you can more accurately target corrective efforts that fit the problem or recognize potentially effective actions through your own readings and research.

Specific Procrastination Styles

Procrastination comes about for different reasons. Like clothing, it comes in different styles. If you know your procrastination style(s), you can mate your corrective efforts to it. This is a big benefit. When you carefully target your corrective actions, you are less likely to go down dead-end streets or invest time in diversions that you may mistake for interventions. Lying on an analyst's

TABLE 1.1

Procrastination Styles and Corrective Actions

Procrastination Style	Awareness and Action Model
Behavioral procrastination occurs when you plan, organize, and initiate actions, then quit prematurely and don't gain the anticipated benefits. For example, over time, you gather materials for 42 different potential hobbies, and the materials are now crowding your storage areas. Your company conducts meetings to explore different marketing opportunities, but follow-up beyond the exploratory stage is rare.	*Awareness:* Do you tend to start projects, then leave them undone? If so, what are they? Where, how, and why do you stop yourself? *Action:* Select two projects that you have a high probability of starting and finishing. Construct a plan to get through the bottleneck. Address any urge to diverge as you execute the plan and come to a point where you'd ordinarily stop.
Health procrastination is putting off making, executing, or maintaining healthy choices. Delays in this area may have tragic results that affect both your work and your life. Within three years, about 50 percent of those who have coronary bypass operations stop taking medication and revert to the same habits that initially got them into trouble. People who gain excess weight are at high risk for health problems. Exercise may be the best antidepressant, but it is also infrequently employed.	*Awareness:* Do you avoid regular medical or dental examinations, eating healthily, or exercising regularly? If so, what do you tell yourself to support your health procrastination? *Action:* What purpose would taking positive health actions serve for you? What three concrete productive actions would you be willing to take now to address health procrastination? When will you start?
Reactance procrastination is a form of resistance toward the removal of a perceived right, convenience, or privilege. You may think, feel, and act rebellious when faced with conditions that you believe threaten this freedom. You rebel against any suggestion that you drink too much. Deadlines interfere with other activities that you'd prefer, and so you try to get around the deadlines. You enjoy your daily quart of ice cream and resent following a medical recommendation to lose weight by cutting back on it.	*Awareness:* What is the major area in your life where you resist useful changes to avoid losing an unhealthy privilege? *Action:* Do a quick long-term advantage-disadvantage analysis. What are the long-term advantages of continuing a harmful habit? What are the long-term disadvantages? How do these add up?

TABLE 1.1 (continued)

Procrastination Style	Awareness and Action Model
Change procrastination is avoiding change. This frequency of this reaction increases when you face uncertainties, you feel awkward, or your ego gets in the way. Change procrastination may overlap with reactance procrastination when you resent dropping one thing to do another, or when the change challenges a traditional view that you are reluctant to give up.	*Awareness:* What situations do you back away from to suppress feeling uncertain? What do you tell yourself to justify the delay? *Action:* Since change is inevitable, what three changes do you back away from that you can benefit from making? What three techniques have you read about that you believe you can apply to support making these changes?
Lateness procrastination can be a challenging habit to break. You habitually show up late for meetings, appointments, and social events. This procrastination style has characterizing features. When the time comes for you to leave for meetings or appointments, you make phone calls, shower, and look for missing paperwork, and so the list goes on.	*Awareness:* If you have a habit of starting late, what purpose does this delaying action serve? Does it continue because it has gone on before? *Action:* What's your incentive to act to change the pattern? Leave a message on your own answering unit describing steps you should take so as not to start late. Then listen to the message one hour before the time comes to depart.
Learning procrastination, and its subvariety academic procrastination, refers to avoiding study and learning. Like many other procrastination subvarieties, learning procrastination is a complex procrastination style that can occur at work, at school, and at home. How about that book you bought on plumbing that is gathering dust?	*Awareness:* Where can you most profit from advancing your knowledge through study but don't follow through? How do you get in your own way and stop yourself from studying? *Action:* Interact with learning information as often as you can. Make it concrete. Make it applicable. Put three methods on a wallet-sized card that reminds you how to handle procrastination urges, thinking, and behavioral divergences when you are about to engage in study.

TABLE 1.1 (continued)

Procrastination Style	Awareness and Action Model
Promissory note procrastination is a form of personal procrastination in which you make promises to yourself that you'll take action to improve what you've already put off. A classic example is making a New Year's resolution and then not following through.	*Awareness:* What changes have you promised yourself that you'd make that are important for you to accomplish? What excuses do you make to sanitize delaying certain actions that are in your best interests? *Action:* On a five-point scale, with one representing fact and truth and five distortion and misrepresentation, at what point in the scale do your excuses lie? If your excuses are largely invalid, develop an action plan to take concrete steps to fulfill your commitment to yourself.
Faffing procrastination is what the word implies. This is aimlessly frittering away time on useless activities, or appearing to look busy but producing little to nothing of value. In faffing procrastination, you complain about being busy, busy, busy, and that's why you are behind. Busy, busy, busy, *but* busy doing what?	*Awareness:* If you find yourself going around in circles doing one busy activity after another without getting anywhere, what do you tell yourself to perpetuate this busyness myth? *Action:* Reflect and identify three weak points in the faffing process, such as believing that busywork is the same as productive achievements. Target a real achievement. Refuse to engage in faffing diversions. Take one hour a day to pursue your most ambitious and productive goal.

TABLE 1.1 (continued)

Procrastination Style	Awareness and Action Model
Disapproval avoidance procrastination refers to a habit of avoiding disapproval by playing it safe, avoiding conflict through appeasement, and avoiding actions or situations that could lead to criticism. Blame avoidance procrastination is sometimes present as well. Self-protection is common. However, avoiding disapproval is practically impossible. The cost in lost opportunities tends to be steep.	*Awareness:* It's normal to want to get along with others. However, do you bend over backward to avoid disapproval at significant personal cost? Do you avoid standing up for your rights and procrastinate on making efforts to learn appropriate assertive skills? *Action:* Consider what you want to accomplish in your interpersonal relations. If your goal is to feel like you are on an equal footing with others, then what steps can you take to curb procrastination on learning to be authentically self-expressive?
Blame avoidance procrastination. We live in a blame culture, where blame and blame avoidance are normally a big issue. In blame avoidance procrastination, you avoid situations that could result in criticism, and you seek to cover up for perceived faults and failings. Blame is intended to maintain a positive public image. Blame avoidance activities include such things as finger-pointing, spin control, cover-up activities, loophole seeking, and excuse making. Organizations are hotbeds of blame avoidance activities.	*Awareness:* If we stuck with blame as a means of assigning responsibility, we'd need fewer lawyers. Nevertheless, blame is a common factor in organizations, and a better way to avoid blame is to keep moving ahead while others procrastinate. *Action:* Think about areas where you can assert control over your work and develop yourself into an expert in those areas. You'll have less concern about blame. When you invest time in developing your competencies, your work value increases, and blame is less likely. An elegant solution is to defend your positions without having to defend yourself, to act to give yourself unconditional self-acceptance.

couch to free-associate about early childhood issues about procrastination can be a diversion. Table 1.1 describes a sample of procrastination styles and corrective actions.

Procrastination styles may surface in different contexts and have some unique twists. However, the underlying procrastination processes are roughly comparable. Thus, when you understand this underlying process, you can use this knowledge to address procrastination across a variety of contexts and styles.

Self-Absorbed versus Self-Observant Perspectives

Acknowledging a procrastination habit is a critical step on the path to change. Having some preexisting knowledge of what lies on the path is better yet. You'll know where to look and what to target. Even if you don't have an interest in tackling procrastination now, understanding how the process works may later lead you to experiment with counter-procrastination ideas and techniques.

Moving from a procrastination path to a productive one often starts with a shift *from* feeling absorbed in procrastination process thinking, feeling, and behaving *to* a self-observant problem-solving perspective. When you are self-absorbed, you draw inward. You're concerned about how you feel, how you might look to others, or whether you are perfect enough. When you are absorbed in such anxious thoughts and feelings, you may find it hard to keep your productive goals in focus. Procrastination thoughts may linger as you languish. This inward view finds outward expression in procrastination.

A self-observant way of knowing and doing involves a radical shift from an inward to a reality perspective that is elegant in its simplicity:

1. Monitor your thoughts, feelings, and actions and do a perception check.

2. Take a scientific approach, in which you rely on observation and draw evidence-based inferences and conclusions.
3. Predict the outcome of playing out different scenarios.
4. Act rationally to achieve enlightened positive goals.
5. Learn from planned procrastination countermeasures and apply new learning.

On a case-by-case basis, you can make a radical shift from a self-absorbent to a self-observant perspective. Unlike learning to read, where it takes several years to get the basics and to build from there, you can start this shift right away. However, progressive mastery of procrastination is a process that extends over a lifetime but gets simpler and easier in time. As the rewards for your self-observant efforts pile up, you'll have added incentive to continue in this do-it-now way.

Keep a Procrastination Log to Boost Your Awareness

A procrastination log is an awareness tool for tracking what you do when you procrastinate. Logging what you think, how you feel, and what you do as you procrastinate promotes metacognitive awareness. This is your ability to think about your thinking and to make connections between your thoughts, emotions, behaviors, and results. If you prefer a more freewheeling style, create a narrative in which you log an ongoing commentary of what is happening when you procrastinate.

When you have an impulse to delay, start recording and logging what you tell yourself and how you feel. Note the diversionary actions that you take. If you are unable to make immediate recordings, record procrastination events as soon as you are able to do so, and be as concrete and specific as you can about what you recall observing.

You may find it equally important to record what you think, feel, and do when you follow through. What can you learn from your follow-through actions that you can apply to procrastination situations?

By nailing down what goes on when you procrastinate, you put yourself in the catbird seat to understand the process and disrupt it with a do-it-now alternative action. However, personal change is ordinarily a process, not an event. It takes experimenting and time to test and integrate new self-observant ways of thinking, feeling, and doing. The new habits will compete with a practiced self-absorbent procrastination style that may carry on as though it had a life of its own. However, once you are into a process of change, you may find building on the process easier and simpler.

From Procrastination to Productivity: The Five Phases of Change

The five phases of the change process are awareness, action, accommodation, acceptance, and actualization. I first used this structure for change in my early seminars and group counseling sessions with people who wanted to stop procrastinating. The process assumes a self-observant perspective. It is a way to organize a counter-procrastination program into a powerful process.

In this dynamic system for change, the different phases interact. The priority ordering may change. Action may lead to insightful awareness. Accommodation includes seeing incongruities and contradictions and adjusting to reality. Acceptance may make it easier to experiment with new ideas and behaviors. In actualization, you stretch to discover your boundaries, and you may find that you broaden those boundaries the more you stretch. This knowledge adds to a growing awareness of what you can accomplish through your self-regulated efforts. The following describes how the process works.

Phase 1: Awareness

Awareness is listed as the first phase of change. You intentionally work to sharpen your conscious perspective on what is taking place within and around you during procrastination and do-it-now approaches to problems. You apply what you learned about making a radical shift from a self-absorbent to a self-observant perspective. You think about your thinking. You make your goals clear to yourself. As a means of self-discovery through productive efforts, you guide your actions through self-regulatory thoughts to discover what you can do to reduce procrastination by increasing your efforts to promote productive actions.

Positive Actions for Change. On a situation-by-situation basis, map and track what you do when you procrastinate. Identify what is similar and what is different from situation to situation. Connect the dots between do-it-now activities and procrastination and outcome factors. These may include type and quality of accomplishment. Ask yourself the following questions:

- What type of stress do you experience when you are in a do-it-now mode of operating? (This usually involves a productive form of stress, or p-stress.)
- What type of stress do you experience the longer you put off a pressing and important activity? (Procrastination tends to be coupled with various forms of distress, or d-stress.) What do you conclude from this information?

Phase 2: Action

Action is your experimental component for change. You actively test ideas to see what you can do to promote visible products from your work efforts and conceptual and emotional changes from reflecting on the process that you used to produce positive results. In this stepping-stone phase, you put one foot in front of the other to test your ideas against reality. While words in books on how to drive a car can tell you what to do, really learning to do starts by getting behind the wheel. You may never be a perfect driver, but through practice and experience, you can develop the skill to be a competent driver. Conquering procrastination starts in a similar way. You may never be perfectly productive, but you can be competent in the area of self-learning and development. By initiating concrete actions, you are likely to gain productive ground.

Positive Actions for Change. Awareness is the first step listed. However, it isn't necessarily the first step to take. By accidental discovery, an action can prompt a new awareness. You can enter the process of change at any point, such as experimenting with do-it-now actions to see what you can learn about yourself as the agent of change in this process. Advance the nonfailure concept from the Introduction by framing proposed actions as hypotheses. Like a scientist, you test whether an action you have decided on will promote a desired outcome.

- Make a contract with yourself to perform prescribed steps to introduce a change in the procrastination process. Instead of following an urge to diverge, live with the urge for five minutes and observe what happens. What did you learn?
- After examining the urge for five minutes, act to follow do-it-now steps. What happened? What did you learn?

Phase 3: Accommodation

Accommodation is the cognitive integration phase of change. It's my favorite part of the process. Here you play with juxtapositions, incongruities, and paradoxes between productive and procrastination points of view. For example, tomorrow views and do-it-now views have many contradictions. You don't *do it now* tomorrow.

Positive Actions for Change. Accommodating new ways of thinking, feeling, and acting first involves testing new feelings, thoughts, and actions. It normally takes a while for the brain to adjust to new ways of thinking, feeling, and behaving.

- Contrast procrastination and do-it-now views. What do you gain by thinking that later is better? What do you gain by following a do-it-now path? What makes later seem so hopeful when reality tells a different story?
- Is it possible to change procrastination goals to avoid effort and work to productive goals? Can the productive goal include observing a strong procrastination process to identify its weaknesses and vulnerabilities?
- Can you convert complaints that support procrastination to positive goals? For example, "This is too complicated for me" may be converted to "I can handle the first step." If you first see an action as too complicated, yet you can handle the first step, you've found a procrastination paradox.
- If you tell yourself that you work better under pressure, why not plan to put something off until the very last minute? If you tell yourself that you work better under pressure and then swear that you won't put yourself through this type of emotional wringer again, can you have it both ways?
- What might you learn by locating and examining procrastination paradoxes? An example of a procrastination paradox is that you work better under pressure, yet you want to work smarter next time by starting earlier. The odds are that you don't work better under pressure; rather, you are more likely to start when you feel pressured.

Phase 4: Acceptance

Acceptance is the phase of change in which you take reality for what it is, not what you think it ought to be. Acceptance supports tolerance, and this frees up energy that is ordinarily sopped up by blame and doubts and beliefs that promote fears. Acceptance is cognitive, but it is also an emotional integration phase of change. Acceptance has a quieting effect, but also a positive energizing effect when you translate this view into a willingness to experiment and satisfy your curiosity about how far you can stretch and grow.

Positive Actions for Change. Acceptance involves the recognition of variability. What parts of your life are working well, and what have you done to establish that state? In what phases of your life do you fall short of ably regulating your actions? Is it possible for you to accept this state and still consider productive actions to improve your condition? Ask yourself these additional questions:

- If you procrastinate, so be it. Now, what can you do to change the pattern and get better if you choose to do so?
- Do you live in a pluralistic world that involves adaptability to different situations or a world in which a systematic and procedural approach and scheduling resolve all difficulties? Is there room for both views?
- What have you learned from considering this emotional integration phase of change?

END PROCRASTINATION NOW! TIP
The CHANGE Plan

Conquer a procrastination challenge by breaking it down to manageable parts.

Hang in with your positive do-it-now plan until it becomes automatic.

Adapt to altering conditions while keeping your eye on opportunities to follow a do-it-now plan.

Negate distractions by acting on what is most important and pressing to do.

Gain from the experience by reviewing what you did well that you can repeat.

Envision your next do-it-now steps to move forward to achieve new productive goals.

Phase 5: Actualization

Actualization is often portrayed as a mysterious process in which you have oceanic or peak experiences. It may be a Buddha-like desireless state. It may be a state of mind in which you experience a conceptual and emotional sense of connectedness with all of humanity across cultures, time, and dimension. You can also view actualization as stretching your abilities and resources enough to promote meaningful changes in your life in those areas where such efforts are meaningful and important. That's how I prefer to use the concept.

Positive Actions for Change. Follow-through is to actualization as water is to plant growth. What actions can you take to rescript your life narrative to include the results of experiments in stretching to find the boundaries of what you are able to accomplish that you'd value? Additional questions to ask yourself are:

- What ideas or actions have you found effective in one phase or zone of your life that you can apply to procrastination zones where you are experiencing stagnation?
- Does organizing and regulating your ideas and actions promote stretching and accomplishing?
- What do you learn about yourself by taking a few extra steps to stretch in the direction of actualization?

Change can be something you just do. Let's say you want to alter your appearance to initiate change, or maybe you'd like to take a vacation for a change. But some changes take time and a process that can compete with an old habit that you wish to change.

Changing from a pattern of delays to a productive pattern is rarely a finger-snapping act. Getting yourself disentangled from the cognitive, emotive, and behavioral dimensions of procrastination typically takes a process of pitting reason against the unreason of procrastination thinking, learning to tolerate tension without easily giving in to urges to diverge, and establishing behavioral patterns where you act against behavioral diversions by engaging in productive actions.

In working through this process—and as you practice, practice, practice—there will come a time when you'll find yourself shifting your efforts into productive pursuits as automatically as you once avoided many of them. You can apply the five phases of change again and again to help promote that outcome.

The French psychologist and educator Jules Payot thought, "The aim of the great majority is to get through life with the least possible outlay of thought." If you want to differentiate yourself from others immediately, start a course of voluntary change in which you reach out and expand your capabilities to overcome procrastination!

Voluntary actions for personal change may be among the challenging variety. That's because there may not be a clear starting point. There are no deadlines because the change is an ongoing lifetime process. The process involves self-observant directed effort. This effort is a necessary step. Have you ever accomplished something of merit without effort? It is your turn next to test the process to see if you can change procrastination events:

Positive Change Actions
Awareness:
Action:
Accommodation:
Acceptance:
Actualization:

Mythologist and Columbia University Professor Joseph Campbell saw this pattern in tales of heroes. There is a challenge. An ally fills in information. The hero discovers how to apply the knowledge. Are you up to the challenge?

End Procrastination Now! Your Plan

Change, even the most positive kind, normally involves periods of adjustment and accompanying stress. When you anticipate changing a practiced routine, this anticipation can evoke stress. You might procrastinate. If you view some discomfort as a natural part of life and change, you are more likely to progress.

What three ideas for dealing effectively with procrastination have you had? Write them down.

1.

2.

3.

What are the top three actions that you can take to shift from procrastination toward productive action? Write them down.

1.

2.

3.

What things have you done to execute your action plan? Write them down.

1.

2.

3.

What things did you learn from applying your ideas and action plan that you can use? Write them down.

1.

2.

3.

2

Defeat Procrastination Thinking

In *The Folly of Procrastination*, first published in the 1800s, the unnamed author tells of two young brothers, Edward and Charles Martin. One procrastinated; the other didn't. Edward started his work early and finished early. Charles marched to a different tune. After school, he put his books aside and told himself, "Oh, there is time enough; I'll learn my lessons this evening." Then he started to play. When evening came, he felt sleepy and told himself, "Oh, I can learn them before school time in the morning." When morning came, Charles put it off again. As time ebbed, Charles found that he didn't know where to begin. Nevertheless, he sketched out a few quick answers to his "hated" work and then rushed to school.

The "I'll get to it later" mindset is like a promissory note. It amounts to paying later for the privilege of playing now. However, you will normally find usurious interest charges before and when the loan comes due.

We see this *later illusion* played out in many scenarios, like the workplace, the home, at college—practically any place where you will find procrastination. This thinking serves as a cognitive diversion because it detours you away from the pressing activity, along what seems like a safer path.

Like a chameleon, procrastination thinking may change with the type of delay and where it happens. Professors who put off writing articles may say, "I had to do more research." In a business setting, you may hear, "I had too many e-mail messages that I had to answer." You may hear passive-voice explanations, such as, "People were slow getting back to me." The passive voice can be like a cloaking device to hide the specific reasons for the delay.

When procrastination is on the move, self-cons are not far behind. You think, "I deserve a rest, and will get to it later." When you keep these diversions to yourself, they normally go unchecked.

Join me as we explore how you can defeat procrastination thinking. Together we'll look at the forms this thinking takes, where it leads, and your options for changing the process. Let's start with examples of procrastination thinking. After that, you'll find multiple solutions for putting this thinking to rest while you go about operating like the efficient and effective person you know you have the power to be.

Types of Procrastination Thinking

The singer/actor Dean Martin captured the spirit of *later thinking* in the song *Manaña*. In this song, Martin sings about a broken window, a dripping faucet, and other results of procrastination. He repeated a line saying that "manaña is soon enough" for him. The lyricist understood the effects of a classic form of procrastination thinking. Not much gets done when later seems better.

Procrastination thinking is a mental diversion, or a way of sidestepping a timely and important activity. This kind of thinking has different twists, but the message is the same. Thoughts like "I need to let the idea simmer longer" or "I'll get to it after I take a nap and feel rested" probably signal that procrastination is in process. And while taking a nap may be a good idea if you are fatigued and can't concentrate, it gets suspicious if, on the way to your nap, you perk up if you have a chance to talk with a friend.

"I'll Do It Tomorrow" Thinking

The mañana trap is elaborate. However, you might take this thinking to another level. Under the cloak of "I'll do it tomorrow" thinking, you make one task dependent on doing another first. Then you put off the contingent activity. With this form of conditional thinking, you can chain one contingency onto another and delay them all.

You want to get an MBA degree. You can see the benefits, and you want them. You think the knowledge you will get from the courses and the status you will get from the degree will open a promising career track and you can get a significant pay raise. However, you tell yourself that first you need to gather and digest information about every possible MBA program to make sure that you are getting the best program possible. Then you put off gathering the material. When you get it, you put off reading it. That's the beauty of a contingency mañana plot. By finding new diversions, you avoid the challenge.

In another form of contingency thinking, you make feeling motivated and inspired the contingency. Feeling good is your green light for action. So, unless your back is to the wall, you'll be tempted to put off doing anything unless you feel good about doing it.

As another emotional contingency, you wait for a moment of inspiration to get started. But who expects to be inspired to file work orders? It's not that feeling good about what you do is a problem. The problem is delaying action while passively awaiting an unpredictable emotional state. From time to time, you'll experience an emotional state in which your problems are manageable, you are unaffected by negative events, and you efficiently finish what you would ordinarily put off. Thus, there is a basis for saying that you do better when you are inspired. How often does that happen?

The Backward Ploy

In the *backward ploy*, you tell yourself that before you can defeat procrastination, you need to know how you came to procrastinate.

Otherwise, you're doomed to repeat the pattern. You tell yourself that until you get around to this archaeological expedition into the depths of your psyche, you'll never be free from procrastination. Meanwhile, you have a perfect excuse for procrastinating forever.

This ploy can have the surface appearance of seeking deep answers to profound questions about the self. It can sound like a sophisticated act. Yet it serves the same purpose as the other contingency ploys: avoidance, avoidance, avoidance.

There is no compelling evidence that scientifically demonstrates that searching through incomplete and biased memories to reach premapped but speculative unconscious territories correlates with reducing procrastination. However, understanding what you do today to create needless delays can be productive. Recognizing procrastination thinking, for example, opens an opportunity to change your thinking and get under way with what is important to do now.

Self-Handicapping and Procrastination

Self-handicapping is a term coined by psychologists Edwin Jones and Steven Berglas; it describes a cognitive process of enhancing self-esteem in dealing with tasks or goals that you may or may not be good at. Self-handicapping plays a critical role in your procrastination process. By laying the blame on uncontrollable obstacles, you can save face when you deliver subpar or failing performances. You have to take your hat off to anyone who creates this no-lose form of self-protection. However, does it come with a price? The price is likely to be in the direction of procrastination and mediocrity.

Here is how self-handicapping can feed procrastination. Your boss explains that because the economy is tight, your new assignment is to renegotiate purchasing contracts with the company's suppliers. She wants to put the company into a better competitive position by reducing prices without affecting profit margins. She thinks this is an opportunity to increase market share.

You think something else. You might be able to pull this off, but you are doubtful. Instead of facing your insecurities about your ability to negotiate a price reduction, you tell yourself—and others—that your boss is being unrealistic. The suppliers won't budge on price. So, based on that self-protective assumption, you drag your feet on setting up meetings, make a halfhearted effort to negotiate, and fulfill the prophecy. You reinforce your belief that your boss was unrealistic.

Handicapping is common in organizational settings. You can say that you could have done your work on schedule if you had had better people, more money, active cooperation from superiors, and more hours in the day. Office politics are distractions, as are complaints that others have not done their part, or that you were thrown off because you didn't have the supplies in time, or that the computer had glitches, or that the company consultants were messing with the system. If you are in a position where you'd compete with a more skilled player, might you handicap yourself by telling yourself that you don't stand a chance?

Why would a reasonable person consciously or subconsciously seek ways to promote a decrease in productive performances through self-handicapping? The usual suspects are social anxieties and fears about disappointing others, disapproval (evaluation anxiety), image management, and expediency (going for a quick way to avoid or shed tension).

The self-handicapping trap has an easily picked lock. If you want to spring yourself, you might consider evoking the concept of nonfailure and ask yourself the following questions:

- *Which of your personal resources can you apply to take the first step?* Think about your thinking. Are you setting yourself up to procrastinate by prejudging a situation as too tough, complicated, unpleasant, or undoable? If so, introduce a change into this thinking process. First, ask and answer what makes the task too tough for *you?* Separate belief and assumption from fact. Consider the Chinese philosopher Lao-tzu's (604–531 BC) oft-quoted perspective that the journey of a thousand miles begins beneath your feet.

- *Is self-handicapping inconsistent with your expressed long-term goals?* If so, what needs to change? What can you do to prepare differently in the next situation where self-handicapping beliefs surface and fog reality? For example, by recognizing self-handicapping procrastination thinking as a consistent but correctable error, you've put a special form of procrastination thinking into the spotlight.

- *Will awareness alone thwart a self-handicapping process?* Awareness is a start. You can normally advance this awareness by contrasting handicapping self-statements with do-it-now thinking and behavior. We'll get into how to create and support a productive do-it-now idea later in this chapter.

Counterfactual Thinking

Counterfactual thinking is about what didn't happen but could have happened had you acted differently. One form is an *upward counterfactual* because it points to what you could have done to promote a better outcome. This thinking can extend into self-recrimination if you tend to blame yourself, or it can be useful information for future planning.

If there is an upward counterfactual, you can bet that you can find a *downward counterfactual.* This is about what could have been worse had you not acted as you did.

Unless you are careful about upward counterfactuals, you may get down on yourself. If you allow for no past, present, or future errors, counterfactual thinking can be a terror. If hindsight turns into an examination of what you should have had the foresight to see, this view can be dysfunctional

Downward counterfactuals are upward in the sense that you both have distanced yourself from the event and can feel better because things could have been worse.

You may feel better about your performance with a downward counterfactual than with an upward counterfactual. For example, Olympic silver medalists are inclined to occupy themselves with what they could have done to get the gold, and bronze medalists tend to think about their good fortune in avoiding fourth place.

Upward counterfactual thinking is associated with higher levels of procrastination under anxious circumstances. When counterfactuals combine with self-handicapping, the trend is to excuse procrastination and improve self-esteem. When delays lead to weak performance, safeguarding one's image can come into play in two ways: "If only I hadn't procrastinated on preparing for my presentation, I would have gotten the promotion." This combination makes performance improvements less likely.

Depending on the situation, *could have* thinking can have different effects. This thinking can be depressing if you believe that you are powerless to take corrective actions in the next situation. You might consider how to do better in the future, and plan for taking the types of actions that offer you the best chance. Downward counterfactuals can help you save face. You have better alternatives.

- The first century AD Roman Emperor Marcus Aurelius said: "Your past is gone, your future is uncertain." If you take this message to heart, you know that you cannot change what has been done, but that the corrective actions you take today apply to shaping a positive future.
- "Could have" counterfactuals are associated with higher levels of procrastination. It doesn't have to be that way. With reflection and planning, you could have fewer "could haves" and more "have done" experiences.
- You can turn counterfactual thinking, such as "I could have done better," into corrective reflection. If a counterfactual follows a delayed effort, use the occasion to plan a promising new counter-procrastination strategy. What do you want to

accomplish? What steps can you take to improve? When will you take them? How will you measure the results? How will you know when to adjust the plan?

- You can have the best analysis and plan possible, but you won't get beyond the joys of mental preparation unless you convert the plan into action. How might procrastination get in the way of a solution for curbing procrastination? What are you prepared to do to short-circuit mental and behavioral diversions?

Procrastination thinking is an automatic habit, but once you are aware of your automatic procrastination thinking habit, you are in a position to disengage from it. Here are some tips for deflating automatic procrastination thinking: (1) monitor your thinking, (2) identify the mental diversion, (3) question it, and (4) force yourself to follow through.

The ABCDE Method for Altering Procrastination Thinking

More than any psychology self-help system builder, New York psychologist Albert Ellis drew core principles from Epictetus' philosophy and built them into a powerful rational emotive behavior therapy (REBT) approach. You can apply the method to decrease stress, promote wellness, and end procrastination.

Research into the complexity of human nature and REBT methods supports the effectiveness of this foundation method for the cognitive behavioral approach.

You can teach yourself to use Ellis's famous ABCDE approach to attack procrastination thinking. The system delivers a framework for organizing information about procrastination and describes how to challenge and change procrastination thinking. Here's the model:

- **A** stands for an aversive or activating event; it can range from giving up your favorite treats in order to lose weight, to a career reversal, to managing a difficult project.
- **B** refers to what you believe about the A. Beliefs include evaluations and can range from dispassionate to alarming. They usually come in irrational and rational forms. Irrational procrastination beliefs include later thinking. Rational beliefs may include do-it-now thinking. How you go about resolving a conflict between later and do-it-now thinking will help determine whether you will tend to move along a procrastination path or go a do-it-now way.
- **C** refers to the emotional and behavioral consequences that are the by-product of a belief about an unpleasant upcoming responsibility.
- **D** stands for disputing procrastination thinking and replacing these thoughts with fact-based rival beliefs.
- **E** is the socially and personally desirable effect from questioning, challenging, and disputing procrastination thinking.

By questioning procrastination thinking, you help make this type of thinking less automatic. The questions that have the most impact are (1) specific and require concrete answers: when, where, what, and how of experiencing, (2) scientific because they require a concrete answer, and (3) open-ended and flexible to pull more than one answer. The following questions apply to disputing procrastination later thinking:

- *Later Thought:* I'll call home now and worry about getting the schedule done after that.

  Sample question: What would be the result of writing out the schedule now and calling home later?

  Sample answer: I'll have broken a link in the procrastination chain and will have gotten the task off my back.

- *"I'll do it tomorrow" excuse:* I'll deal with my job stresses after I research the subject.

    Sample question: What actions can I take to deal with job stress as I do the research?

    Sample answer: I can start immediately and use the results of my stress reduction efforts to shape what I research next.

In the D phase, you refine your critical-thinking skills by applying them to procrastination thinking.

There is an almost endless number of questions that you can apply to recognize and uproot procrastination thinking. What do you tell yourself or believe about the target situation? Does this belief represent an assumption or a fact? Is there credible evidence to support the way you view the situation? Can you treat your belief like a hypothesis and test it? Do these questions help promote a realistic perspective?

If you prefer to use a tested set of questions, the following cookbook approach can serve that purpose. Here you apply six standards for rational thinking that you can contrast with suspected stress thinking and what you believe are examples of do-it-now thinking (see Table 2.1).

Your answers to these questions become disputes against the irrationalities of procrastination thinking. Additionally, the act of pausing and reflecting to interrupt an impulsive procrastination reaction introduces a change into the system to check your thinking about the situation.

Now let's take a look at the following ABCDE example, which shows how to use a do-it-now perspective to counteract procrastination thinking. Do you remember the example of Jane's procrastination pattern from the introduction? Let's see how she used the ABCDE approach.

Jane's procrastination pattern started when she saw her quarterly financial report assignment as complicated, difficult, and uncomfortable to do. Despite having done similar reports before,

TABLE 2.1

Questions Concerning Different Perspectives

Procrastination Perspective

Do Procrastination Diversionary Actions and Thinking:	Yes	No
1. Fit with reality and personal values?		
2. Promote high-quality performance?		
3. Support relationships among people who depend upon responsible actions?		
4. Allow for a wide range of healthy emotions?		
5. Promote healthy lifestyle habits?		
6. Result in openness to experience and flexibility under changing conditions?		

Do-It-Now Perspective

Does Following Through in a Reasonable Way within a Reasonable Time:	Yes	No
1. Fit with reality and personal values?		
2. Promote high-quality performance?		
3. Support relationships among people who depend upon responsible actions?		
4. Allow for a wide range of healthy emotions?		
5. Promote healthy lifestyle habits?		
6. Result in openness to experience and flexibility under changing conditions?		

she habitually approached each new report with uncertainty and anxiety about her ability to perform effectively. She did a discomfort-dodging waltz by mowing the lawn and hobnobbing. She experienced relief when she decided to delay. She also felt satisfaction from delaying her goal by chatting with a neighbor.

Whatever immediate relief Jane felt was followed by more pressured stress. She heard a nagging inner voice about the delay. She hated this messenger of stress, but felt that she was stuck with it.

When the deadline neared, Jane could delay no longer and still keep her job. She went into a panic mode. She made an eleventh-hour rush. She didn't make the deadline, excused her delay, and got an extension. She lamented that she could have done better had she started earlier. However, history repeated itself when she found herself in similar circumstances. Here is what she did to break this procrastination pattern through the ABCDE approach.

Jane's *A* was the impending deadline for her financial report. She thought of the report as complex and difficult. She was uncertain about where to begin, and so she scurried around the issue while hoping for inspiration. Jane had expectations of perfection, and her self-doubts partially resulted from her fear that she wasn't as capable as she thought she should be. She evaluated the project as threatening. She evaluated the tension she experienced as unbearable. Thus, her procrastination was complex.

It's normally unrealistic to handle all the ingredients that go into a complex procrastination pattern simultaneously. This is like trying to read a book while driving. So, Jane started by working through her tomorrow thinking using Ellis's ABCDE approach as her guide. She challenged herself to (1) isolate the later thinking that existed within her, (2) use a do-it-now perspective to introduce a rival belief into the process, and (3) control her impressions through working to develop a realistic outlook about the report.

In the ABC phase of this process, Jane mapped what was going on when she procrastinated. Once she had mapped the process, she was now in the catbird seat to take a close look at the validity of this phase of her thinking. That takes us to D.

Jane followed Epictetus' serenity approach, controlling impressions to generate a new effect. Because she wasn't initially familiar with the ABC approach, part of coming to grips with her procrastination thinking involved educating herself about the system. She found that the best way to educate herself in its use was by direct application to her most pressing procrastination problem.

Table 2.2 gives Jane's resolution for the *later thinking* part of her procrastination habit.

Albert Ellis's rational emotive system includes active behavioral assignments. Thus, it fits well with a do-it-now philosophy to carry through. The behavioral assignments are a form of *exposure.* This is the gold standard for fighting and overcoming performance anxieties and fear and boosting self-confidence. You are less likely to procrastinate on your behavioral assignments to end procrastination if you genuinely see them as being within your ability to do and control, but you have to stretch a bit. Let's look at what Jane assigned herself as a step to prevent future procrastination on report writing. After she finished the report, Jane prepared herself for the next by addressing her high expectations, doubts, and discomfort-dodging tendencies. She set an early start date to ensure that she'd present a high-quality product. She set intermediate deadlines to help her keep momentum. She set an early deadline. When the next report came due, Jane's boss received it early.

END PROCRASTINATION NOW! TIP
Be Aware of Procrastination Thinking

1. Think about your thinking. Help yourself by labeling your procrastination thinking, as this act can provide a sense of controllability.
2. Introduce a change into the procrastination thinking process by disputing your later thinking.
3. Nip procrastination behavioral diversions in the bud by giving yourself a behavioral assignment for following through with a do-it-now initiative.

Keep a positive momentum by taking proactive coping steps.

TABLE 2.2

Jane's ABCDE Resolution

Adversity or activating event: A financial report with a deadline.
Realistic beliefs: The report is complex and time-intensive, and requires basic writing and financial reporting skills. I have the skills to do well enough with the analysis, organization of the material, and writing. (If Jane stuck with that belief, she'd have no need to deal with emotion-amplifying negative beliefs about the report, or a pattern of putting it off. This counterfactual is useful for future do-it-now applications.)
Emotional and behavioral consequences that may extend from the realistic beliefs: Achieving a coping self-efficacy and completing the report with time to spare.
Belief that triggers procrastination: I'll do it better later.
Emotional and behavioral consequences that extend from procrastination thinking: Initial relief following by self-badgering, amplified stress, and more promises to start later. A pressured last-minute rush and excuses to get an extension.
Disputing (correcting) procrastination-related beliefs:

Questions	Straight Answers	Do-It-Now Strategy
Issue: Does later thinking:		
1. Fit with reality?	1. Later thinking is self-deceptive and blocks positive performance.	1. I can define this as a self-development activity and take a nonfailure approach to starting and working through the report.
2. Support performance?	2. The results speak for themselves. I do little that is constructive, and I languish in misery.	2. I can organize my actions around setting a time to start, sticking with that time, and refusing to go off on tangents.

TABLE 2.2 (continued)

Questions	Straight Answers	Do-It-Now Strategy
3. Support positive actions?	3. Delays that continue to affect other people are likely to put people off.	3. I am likely to get favorable performance reviews and salary increases with timely work submissions.
4. Allow for a broad range of emotions?	4. When I delay, I feel pressured, and my emotions are significantly reduced to stressful.	4. While I can't command stress to stop, I can focus on what I can control.
5. Promote healthy lifestyle habits?	5. Dodging discomfort and making tomorrow promises is nonproductive.	5. Corrective actions involve breaking the activity down into what I do first, second, and so forth. (See Chapter 6 for behavioral actions that support a do-it-now philosophy.)
6. Lead to openness to experience and flexibility?	6. Later thinking leads to entrapment in a rut where I spin my wheels and get nowhere fast.	6. I can choose to correct this thinking. I can look at its results and control what I do to produce a different outcome.

Through following the above approach, Jane established control over a negative procrastination process, and such control is positive. She also took action through proactive coping, which you learn more about in Chapter 4. She engaged in proactive coping when she prepared for the next report by working out her problems and planning action before the time to start. Proactive coping is designed to promote effectiveness and well-being. These results represent the new effects she gained through this exercise.

Now, it is your turn to use the ABCDE system (see Table 2.3).

TABLE 2.3

Your ABCDE Resolution

Adversity or activating event:		
Realistic beliefs:		
Emotional and behavioral consequences that may extend from the realistic beliefs:		
Beliefs that trigger procrastination:		
Emotional and behavioral consequences that extend from procrastination thinking:		
Disputing (correcting) procrastination-related beliefs:		
Questions	**Straight Answers**	**Do-It-Now Strategy**
Issue:		
1. Fit with reality?	1.	1.
2. Support performance?	2.	2.
3. Support positive actions?	3.	3.
4. Allow for a broad range of emotions?	4.	4.
5. Promote healthy lifestyle habits?	5.	5.
6. Lead to openness to experience and flexibility?	6.	6.

Effects: What positive new results did you produce for yourself through this exercise? _____

END PROCRASTINATION NOW! TIP

Few things in life are more important than your sense of command of yourself and over what you do. And when it comes to procrastination, you can control your thoughts, your emotions, and your actions.

Can you reduce procrastination thinking to ashes, and will this be permanent? Unfortunately, the procrastination phoenix will rise again and again unless you persist in directing your actions through guided thoughts and a positive emotional intent. The prescription is simple: simultaneously start and follow through on whatever your most timely activity may be, and then stick with actions to keep procrastination thinking in the background. You'll have many opportunities to practice this process.

End Procrastination Now! Your Plan

What three ideas have you had that you can use to help yourself deal with procrastination thinking effectively? Write them down.

1.

2.

3.

What is your action plan?

What are the three top actions you can take to contend with adversity and propel yourself into positive territory? Write them down.

1.

2.

3.

What did you do to implement each of these actions? Write it down.

1.

2.

3.

What did you learn from applying the ideas and the action plan, and how can you next use this information? Write this down.

1.

2.

3.

PART TWO

The Emotive Approach: Build Emotional Tolerance and Stamina for Unpleasant Tasks

3

Flex Your Emotional Muscle to Overcome Procrastination

Now that we've talked about the cognitive component of procrastination, let's take a look at the second important component of the procrastination process—your emotions. Have you ever had a feeling of anxiety when you were faced with a task, so that you ended up avoiding it? For example, a person may avoid following through on creating performance reviews because he feels anxious about the conflicts that may arise when evaluating employees.

Ending procrastination partially involves building stamina and resiliency, or what I like to call "emotional muscle." With practice and exercise, you can toughen up so that you can withstand your emotional drives to retreat from productive pursuits. However, building emotional muscle is a constructive striving to build on the positive emotional capacities involved in the activation of purposeful and productive efforts to produce and prosper.

Building your emotional muscle when reacting to the anxieties, fears, and unpleasant emotions that cause procrastination will allow to you tolerate the tensions, pressures, and frustrations that take place along the path of life. While you are building emotional muscle, you learn to let go of short-term rewards in favor of larger longer-term gains. You accept life as being neither great nor terrible; rather, it is what it is. Paradoxically, your willingness to accept tension means that you'll have less tension to tolerate. Without the limitations set by tension-driven procrastination, you'll see and have more opportunities. Productive choices are at the gate of those opportunities. As you will see when we move ahead, there are various ways to build your emotional muscle, to strengthen your resolve to get things done.

There are three primary steps on the path of developing emotional muscle:

1. Developing tolerance through acceptance is a step on the path.
2. Reframing ego and discomfort threats as positive opportunities and challenges is a cognitive step on the path.
3. Stretching for excellence, or actualizing your finest abilities, is the third step on the path.

Willpower alone is often not enough to determine the outcome of a conflict within the mind. Instead, our ability to accept a negative affective state is an important start in guiding our behavior away from procrastination tendencies and toward productive activities. Acceptant states of mind are calmer states that are associated with fluidity, flexibility, and productivity. It is simpler and easier to regulate follow-through activities to address issues that trigger the procrastination process. In this chapter, you'll learn about the seductive emotional side of procrastination and how to resist false emotional signals to retreat when it is wiser for you to advance. On this trek you'll:

- See how emotions fuel a procrastination process, and how to redirect those emotions to a productive direction.
- Find a Y condition in productive or procrastination directions, then learn to emphasize the productive direction.

- Discover a simple-easy conflict that can interfere with your productive choices, and learn to see through that conflict.
- Find the key to a double-agenda dilemma that, if left undetected, can leave you baffled why you procrastinate when you tell yourself you want to go a different way. You'll learn to redirect your efforts by putting the emphasis on the right syllable.
- Use a cognitive action exercise for putting the dilemma into perspective and giving weight to a realistic view.
- Learn how to free yourself from procrastination impulses and put yourself on a purposeful and productive cognitive, emotive, and behavioral path by slowing down, creating a productive perspective, and acting on that perspective.

Emotional Procrastination

Procrastination has a strong emotional component. I've seen hundreds of people who complained about their procrastination who either don't tune into their procrastination emotions, recoil from them, or ignore them. Emotional conditions associated with forms of procrastination are varied and complicated, and in the following I point to some of these complications:

- You may get emotional signals following perceptions of upcoming productive activities that you view as ego-threatening (a threat to your sense of worth or image) or uncomfortable. These threat sensations can range from whispers of unpleasant emotions to a distinctive emotion of anxiety or fear. Either the whisper of unpleasant emotion or the emotion may be sufficient to divert you from the activity you connect to it.
- Procrastination may be affected by mood. Moods are a gray area of consciousness; they can reflect your disposition, your temperament, your circadian rhythms, your sleep patterns, barometric changes, and other such factors. You can create a

mood by what you think and how you view what is upcoming for you to do. A pervasive gray mood may predispose you to avoid some productive activities that you might otherwise engage in.

- We can create emotions through the images we conjure up in our minds. Method actors have known this for more than a century: if you want to feel angry, reconstruct an angry event in your mind. You can also act out pleasant emotions and constructive habits and use these experiments to build confidence in yourself as a change maker.
- Threat and pleasure cognitions stir emotions. These emotive cognitions are caused by what you think. Preexisting moods may influence these interpretations, evaluations, and beliefs. These emotive cognitions interact with behaviors.

Emotions are distinguishable. You know when you're sad, happy, or angered, but emotions can also feel confusing. You can have more than one view of a situation and experience mixed emotions. Some emotions seem so general, persistent, and unpleasant that you may do anything you can to dull them. Emotional procrastination involves avoiding productive situations that you associate with unpleasant emotions. This omission can slow progress. You see complexity, unpleasantness, or threat in various tasks, so you back off from them. For example, do you find yourself putting off things like fixing a leaky faucet, giving bad news, or avoiding someone who will ask you about your progress on a project that you are also putting off? When you retreat, you act like you were telling yourself that the task is too unpleasant or tough to do right now, but you'll get to it later. When the event, emotion, explanation, and behavioral diversions merge, dealing with these procrastination complications can seem like pulling out the ingredients from a spaghetti sauce. However, that's not so much the case here. Pulling out one area for corrective action may influence the others. The question is where to place the emphasis. When negative emotions spur repeated procrastination performances, emotional procrastination is a prime area to address.

Sensations and Emotions

You may go to a horror movie to experience fear. You gravitate toward people you find attractive. Your favorite comedian is in town, and you go to the show to have a good laugh. You enjoy a good massage, a swim in a lake, a walk through a garden, and a sea breeze against your cheeks. You experience pleasure in finishing a race. You enjoy listening to music before a warm fire. You feel glued to the screen of your TV as the history of planet earth unfolds. Indeed, there are countless emotional and sensory pleasures in life that add to the enjoyment of living.

Emotional states motivate action. If you are curious, you are likely to approach what piques your interest. Love can trigger extraordinary actions—if you have love and passion for a specific task

---

END PROCRASTINATION NOW! TIP
Think about Your Emotional Response

When you catch yourself procrastinating, look at how you're feeling and what you're doing in response to the feeling. Results are ordinarily more important than feelings, which tend to be fleeting. Procrastination is a choice for delaying rather than producing.

By weighing the benefits of acting versus delaying, you've introduced a change into the process and have sharpened your choices. As a by-product of exercising a productivity choice, you strengthen your skills that support future productivity choices. Accept that simple solutions to defeat procrastination are not necessarily easy, but can be made so through practice.

Dealing with necessary inconveniences, uncertainty, and discomfort normally gets easier with practice.

or subject, you are more likely to complete such a task. For example, you look forward to doing things that you find pleasurable, and you may get some things you'd ordinarily delay out of the way if they block the path that you want to travel. On the other hand, if you connect an activity to past distresses, you'll probably approach it more tentatively than you would if you favored the activity. If you view a timely priority as highly unpleasant, uncertain, or threatening, you may avoid it even when this costs you dearly.

A Twofer Process. The *twofer process* is a term that I like to use to describe how, by addressing procrastination at the same time you manage its underlying causes, you get a double gain. This effort supports your long-term efforts to build emotional muscle and to prosper more by procrastinating less.

As you saw in an earlier chapter, deadline procrastination, while important to address, is only the tip of the iceberg. How you manage *you* is the more profitable area to probe. By living through avoidance urges and making productive actions to promote accomplishment, you gain in both meeting your deadlines and developing your emotional muscle.

The Horse and Rider Model for Emotional Procrastination

The horse and rider is a metaphor that I like to use when explaining the procrastination process in the context of the emotive approach. It describes why you may feel tempted to take the path of least resistance on matters that are important to start and finish, but that you also view as unpleasant, threatening, boring, uncertain, or risky.

Taking the road of least resistance usually depends on responding more to impulse than to reason. From a producing and thriving vantage, retreat is normally negative. Your higher mental process may have a better way. How is the conflict between a procrastination retreat and a constructive advance resolved?

The psychoanalyst Sigmund Freud uses the metaphor of a horse and rider to show the endless conflict between impulse and reason. The horse is the impulse. The rider controls reason.

The horse represents our passions and our impulses to avoid tension. The horse knows two things: if something doesn't feel good, move away; if something feels pleasurable, go for it. The horse learns new dangers fast. It is a slow learner when it comes to giving up false fears.

The rider is your higher mental processes. The rider reasons, makes connections, plans, and regulates actions. The rider can be a fast learner about maintaining perspective, solving problems, and anticipating change. When the horse's instincts depart from the rider's awareness of reality, the rider has the ability to restrain the horse, but the horse has a mind of its own.

The horse can be spontaneous. The rider may also act spontaneously, but in different ways. The rider sees humor in incongruity, which is something that the horse can never do. Neither the rider nor the horse wants to experience tension, but the rider will recognize when it's necessary to tolerate tension. The horse may prefer grazing to creating an insightful competitive analysis. The rider's job is to create that analysis and avoid horselike distractions.

The rider has the power of reason. Yet, the rider is not always realistic. You may unintentionally distort reality because of false beliefs, such as thinking that inconvenience is terrible. You can worry about failing. Worry is a form of helplessness in the face of uncertainties that can scare the horse and spur procrastination.

Emotional and mental processes that trigger procrastination are not as deeply embedded and invisible as Freud thought. Rather, they are often at the cusp of consciousness and can be made visible if you know where to look. Information from this book and other cognitive behavioral sources can give you a solid template for knowing what you are looking for when you think about your thinking.

The horse and rider metaphor is an important emotive image to help you keep a perspective on the competition between discomfort-dodging urges and the motivation to produce and thrive. Procrastination may be viewed as a battleground between false threat signals that spur the horse, and the visions of a rational rider to create, progress, and avoid longer-term threats that are beyond the horse's vision.

Part of an enlightened rider's challenge is to recognize and find ways to get past fictional threats and engage in productive activities. Thus, when you catch yourself moving along an avoidance path favored by horse instincts, and this doesn't fit with productive opportunities to prosper, an insightful rider may view the struggle as an opportunity to gain a twofer result: building emotional muscle through producing positive results.

Since the primitive brain is ordinarily a slow learner, patience and persistence will ordinarily get you farther down a path than routinely capitulating to the horse's urges. Thus, when you face a decision between lounging and crafting, this is an opportunity for the rider to grab the reins. The more practice you have in grabbing the reins, the easier it becomes to harness the horse's considerable energies and move in the direction of your goal.

The Y Decision. Not all horse and rider combinations are alike. Some are more sensitive to tension: a twinkle of tension can cause the horse to bolt and follow a path of procrastination, with the rider going along with the galloping horse. Another rider may accept discomfort as unavoidable and not a reason to retreat. There are many variations in between these extremes. Nevertheless, the horse and rider analogy suggests a never-ending struggle between primitive emotional impulses and enlightened cognitive controls, which points to a Y decision.

When you come to a branch in the road where your horse wants to follow the path of least resistance, you face a *Y decision*. You know that following through on your goals can be tough. But you want the result. The *Y choice* is to follow through and be productive, or to go a procrastination way.

Whatever the task or goal, the horse normally chooses what it perceives to be the easier or less threatening path. It will gallop to a field, linger by a brook, or head to the barn. The rider may want to go that way. However, sometimes the horse's impulses are best reined in. You have a competitive analysis to do, and your job depends on getting it done before a deadline. But the horse couldn't care less. It's here that an enlightened rider seizes the opportunity to take charge. Guiding the horse takes a special effort.

The difference between the horse running the show and the rider guiding the action is great. So what happens when the goal of the rider and the direction of the horse are different?

What is the rider's decision?

Y-decision solutions normally represent simple choices. To get and stay healthy, you eat healthy food, engage in physical exercise, and deal with stressful situations quickly. You already have a simple solution to stop procrastinating, right? You *just do it*. However, the simple solution isn't that simple to do. When the horse has its say, the plan can go astray.

A goal doesn't trigger delay as much as what you make of it and feel about it. Define a goal as too complicated, and you've intellectually self-handicapped yourself. Tell yourself it is too tough, and you've emotionally self-handicapped yourself.

Chipping away at procrastination involves applying what you know in order to stay productively engaged in timely priorities without handicapping yourself in the process. This can be a simple thing to do. However, it bears repeating that simple is not necessarily the same as easy.

The seventeenth-century Prussian General Carl von Clausewitz observed that ivory-tower theorists can intellectually complicate a simple strategy and bog themselves down with ineffectual fears because of the uncertainties they create that convert into difficulties involving unforeseen possibilities. In von Clausewitz's view, it is wiser to forge ahead. See with your own eyes. Discover the real complexities.

Without using the term *procrastination*, von Clausewitz described how you can make a simple process seem complicated and unimaginably difficult. This procrastination process cannot be addressed theoretically. You can develop a habit of advancing as a way to habituate to uncertainties, discomfort, and the unexpected.

Atlanta, Georgia, artist and psychotherapist Edward Garcia uses an intellectual and emotional view of complexity that partially explains why change can prove surprisingly challenging. When two views clash, the resolution may lean in the direction of avoidance. Figure 3.1 describes a simple-easy conflict.

Let's say that your goal is to register for a strategic planning course on how to plan major projects. When you have a mental and emotional consistency in favor of executing the plan, you are likely to pursue it. Procrastination is not likely to be an issue. But what if there is an inconsistency? You want to register, but you routinely find reasons to put it off. Does that mean that you don't want to sharpen your strategic planning skills?

Although you'd like to gain the benefits, you believe that learning these skills will feel uncomfortable, you worry that others will know more than you do, and you feel apprehensive when you think that you could make a mistake and look foolish. So, you promise

FIGURE 3.1

The Simple-Easy Conflict

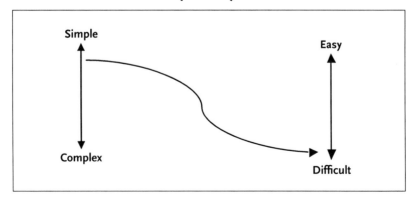

yourself that you'll register later, after you've read a book or two on the topic. Taking the easy route, in this instance, is the emotional goal. It's not that you are secretly against your intellectual goal. Avoiding discomfort as a possible result of your mental projects means more.

Procrastination and the Double-Agenda Dilemma

The double-agenda dilemma is a conflict between stated and implied goals. The first agenda is your stated goals, and this is the rider's interest. You want to register for the strategic planning course. The second agenda is a reflection of the horse's view. You don't want to feel uncomfortable and intellectually inferior. So, essentially, you want the benefits but dislike the process.

With the double-agenda problem, hassle avoidance comes into play in different ways. Hassle avoidance is just what the phrase sounds like: you go out of your way to avoid what you believe is an annoyance or difficulty. Let's say you have a competitive analysis to do and a deadline to make. You'd like to get the analysis done ahead of schedule. You don't like to engage in a process that involves intense concentration. You view the assessment as requiring a lot of concentration. Working at making a competitive analysis takes many steps, including trial-and-error steps and recognizing new opportunities to explore. There is no guarantee that you'll get it completely right. You risk error. The time it takes to do the analysis detracts from pleasurable pursuits. You struggle with reactance, and reactance wins. So, it seems easier to take flight. You start late and barely make the deadline.

You will probably intellectually endorse your stated agenda because it's rational to desire goals that you associate with accomplishment, health, and long-term happiness. Nevertheless, the second agenda may have a greater appeal. So, when you put off a purposeful and productive process, it's not that you don't want the benefits. It's that you want something else more, which is to avoid the complexity or discomfort that goes with the activity.

The double-agenda dilemma comes into play in other ways. Do you eliminate fattening food from your diet now or wait until you've gained 20 more pounds? Do you take steps to act more assertive or continue to act like a doormat? Do you start on your home maintenance to-do list now, or do you wait until the roof starts to leak?

Those who want to get ahead while others procrastinate can be assured that some more talented people are likely to spoil their opportunities by putting their short-term horse interests over their longer-term productive issues. This is sadly true for a subgroup of people who put an enormous amount of time into education and preparation for their careers, only to behaviorally procrastinate when the bigger prizes are within reach.

If you want to meet your first-agenda challenges, but also avoid the uncertainty, difficulty, and discomfort that you associate with the activity, you have a dilemma. You probably can't have it both ways, any more than an alcohol abuser can drink without consequences.

If you didn't experience sensitivity to discomfort and react by retreating, you'd be likely to get more done. However, it is part of the human condition that discomfort signals avoidance. It's easy to fall into a procrastination trap when that happens. But you can learn to use your fast-learning mind to train your slow-learning horse to accept discomfort as part of a process of accruing longer-term benefits. Part of the training is learning to bear discomfort without retreating. Building that stamina is a big part of building emotional muscle.

To resolve a double-agenda dilemma, you face at least three challenges: (1) recognizing the conflict to know what you are up against, (2) applying resources, such as organizing, directing, and regulating your behaviors, to achieve the goal of completing and presenting a competitive analysis, and (3) using your ability to reason, tolerate tension, and act productively to stop discomfort-dodging activities. (If you are interested in learning more about double troubles and its resolution, you can refer to *The Cognitive Behavioral Workbook for Anxiety*.)

Your Short- and Long-Term Analysis

You will often have both intellectual and emotional goals that are related to the same issue. What are your intellectual goals for your most pressing current priority? What are your emotional goals for the same situation? Are you limiting yourself by self-handicapping, counterfactual thinking, rationalizations, and other excuses? Can you find a better way to make your expressed goals the ones you work on to achieve?

When you face uncertainty, associate discomfort with past negative experiences, or just don't like discomfort, your emotional reactions can quickly overpower your reason. For example, you have performance anxiety about giving a marketing presentation before manufacturing. The simple solution is to question your fear thinking and practice speaking in front of groups until you get rid of the anxiety and overcome the fear. If the simple solution was easy, few people would have performance anxiety.

Practically any form of stress can be triggered by something as simple as returning a phone call. Let's assume that the call is to reschedule an appointment. It's not a big deal. You won't seriously inconvenience anyone. You have the time to make the call. But you feel a slight twinge of discomfort. You put off making the call. You tell yourself that you'll get to it later. What went wrong? The horse is running the show.

Let's suppose you recognize the horse's urge to gallop away. Grabbing the reins is a way to change the process. You can grab the reins in many ways, including doing a quick analysis. You may see added benefits from turning things around for yourself.

The following long-term advantage exercise helps strengthen a rider perspective by putting short-term procrastination urges to diverge into a broader context where you can see the frailty in your procrastination reasoning. You are more likely to go for the greater benefit when you write down what you are attempting to accomplish and what you are attempting to avoid.

To complete the short- and long-term procrastination analysis, identify the most pressing and important activity that you are in the process of putting off. Think about both the short- and long-term advantages of delay and then the short- and long-term advantages of the do-it-now way. In short, what do you gain by a pattern of delay? What do you gain by ending procrastination now?

The results of the exercise may be obvious to the rider, but we are talking about reframing the issue to give the rider a tighter grip on the reins. The results of the exercise may trickle down to the horse.

Below you will see an analysis matrix. When you are faced with a task or a goal, think about the long-term and short-term advantages of procrastinating and of doing it now. By completing this exercise you can help yourself tip the balance in favor of going for long-term benefits over short-term rewards. For example, for some people who spent several thousands of dollars on cigarettes, seeing the costs and potential physical/disease consequences in a written matrix format will help them implement corrective actions.

Procrastination Analysis: Advantages

Short-Term	Long-Term
Advantages of procrastination	Advantages of procrastination
Advantages of doing it now!	Advantages of doing it now!

The short-term advantages of a do-it-now initiative may include gaining an initial foothold on a stated productive agenda. The long-term advantages may include (1) progressing toward the goal, (2) building higher levels of frustration tolerance, (3) taking charge of the emotional decision-making process, and (4) less needless stress.

Now, redo the exercise with a different twist. Instead of comparing the advantages of procrastination and stopping procrastination, flip this around and do an analysis of the disadvantages. What are the short- and long-term disadvantages of procrastination and the do-it-now approach?

Procrastination Analysis: Disadvantages

Short-Term	Long-Term
Disadvantages of procrastination	Disadvantages of procrastination
Disadvantages of doing it now!	Disadvantages of doing it now!

This exercise can give you another perspective. The short- and long-term disadvantages of procrastination are typically greater than the benefits.

- Both short- and long-term disadvantages include similar results. The longer-term consequences of repeated procrastination cycles are the more ominous.
- A downside for procrastination is elevating specious relief over long-term benefit.
- Persistent forms of procrastination elevate health risks.
- Omissions in the form of lost opportunities may be a silent but pernicious result of procrastination.
- Delays in promoting productive activity can hinder self-efficacy and negatively affect your self-concept.
- Procrastination that affects others can lead to disgust, hostility, and a loss of credibility.
- Practice procrastination and you'll get better at procrastinating.

The list of short- and long-term advantages from pursuing a do-it-now approach is likely to be short. However, some people view procrastination as something to make light of. There is the laughable pretense by the phony procrastination club that procrastination is an overrated problem. It's fair to say that for some people, procrastination is a serious and complex process. As it is an embedded habit, curbing procrastination takes serious actions. However, these efforts open the gate for new opportunities for productivity, health, and happiness.

The PURRRRS Plan

Procrastination is normally an impulsive response to avoid discomfort. You distract yourself by engaging in substitute activities in order to dodge discomfort. There is a two-phase process for teaching yourself to slow down, understand what is happening, and shift to productive actions. By accepting discomfort, you are less likely to experience discomfort as a trigger for dodging a high-priority activity.

Think of the following PURRRRS exercise as a basic way to slow procrastination impulses, build tolerance for discomfort, and develop permanent cognitive, emotive, and behavioral skills for following through. The following describes the meaning of the acronym.

Pause. This is an awareness phase in which you recognize your
    cues for starting to procrastinate. You tune in to what is
    happening.
Use. You use your cognitive, emotive, and behavioral resources
    to resist the impulse to sidetrack yourself.
Reflect. You probe more deeply into what is happening. What
    are you telling yourself? What are you trying to accomplish?
    What map are you following?
Reason. This includes a consequences analysis. What are the con-
    sequences of following an urge to procrastinate? Do you want
    to change the pattern by promoting the stated over the im-
    plied agenda? What's the action plan for following through?

Respond. This is the execution phase, in which you discover what happens when you think productively, take a no-personal-failure approach, and put yourself on a productive path. At this stage, you put your counter-procrastination plan into action.

Review and revise. This is an assessment phase. You review what you've learned and decide what you can do to improve your counter-procrastination plan.

Stabilize. This is an ongoing phase. You keep practicing and improving your counter-procrastination efforts by actively following a do-it-now path.

The example in Table 3.1 shows how to use PURRRRS to ward off emotional procrastination.

Now that you know how to implement the PURRRRS plan, you can begin using this technique to take a reflective and intentional approach to shifting from following a procrastination impulse to succeeding through productive efforts in which the rider regulates the actions. By repeatedly stopping procrastination with PURRRRS, using Table 3.2, you strengthen your emotional muscle, get more done, and spend less time procrastinating and stressing yourself when you are rushed to finish Once you get used to looking at procrastination through the lens of PURRRS, you'll learn how to mentally and automatically *pause, use, reflect, reason, respond, review,* and *stabilize* to overcome the procrastination habit.

Building Tolerance for Emotional Discomfort

Now that you know how to stop impulsive reactions, you've begun to flex your emotional muscle. Let's take this concept further by learning how to build tolerance for discomfort. How do you build tolerance for discomfort? The answer is partially found by toughing it out to produce results. But since procrastination is a process, and toughing it out with consistency can't be assured, what cognitive-emotive approaches can strengthen the process of building

TABLE 3.1

PURRRRS Planning

Procrastination problem: Putting off completing a competitive analysis.

PURRRRS	Choices Made and Actions Taken
Pause: tune in to what is happening.	Put a green dot on your thumb to remind yourself to tune in to procrastination urges before they cause a shift to e-mailing friends instead of thinking through the problem. This represents the first Y choice: to work on the problem or retreat.
Use cognitive, emotive, and behavioral resources to resist impulses.	This stage involves temporarily living with the discomfort. It's a mobilization stage involving conscious decisions. It represents a second Y choice: staying with the problem or letting the horse race away.
Reflect: think about what is happening.	In this metacognitive phase, you think about your thinking. What does the horse have to say? What is the rider's way? That frames another Y choice: which view has the greater sway?
Reason and plan out your actions.	What are the potential consequences of grabbing the reins? What are the potential consequences of letting the horse bolt? This leads to another Y choice: do you plan to start the project? If so, what is the first step? What are the short- and long-term benefits of these actions? Do you let the horse race away? If so, what is the first step? What are the long- and short-term benefits of these actions?

emotional muscle? How do you translate that tolerance into do-it-now behavioral actions?

- *Tune in to what you tell yourself when you feel discomfort about a productive task.* Is it an urge to avoid or escape it? If you catch yourself thinking, "I don't want to," that may be true. You may not want to study a competitor's marketing approach. Still, if this is a job responsibility, how do you grab the reins and get it done and out of the way?

TABLE 3.1 (continued)

PURRRRS	Choices Made and Actions Taken
Respond by putting your plan into action	In this phase, you face additional Y choices. Do you plan, organize, and start and then behaviorally procrastinate to give the horse the reins? Do you tough it out when the going gets rough by moving forward with the plan?
Review and revise: make adjustments to improve the plan and the results. When warranted, try another way.	Few plans are so great that they are beyond improvement. There will be times where reflective experiences provoke new insights and suggest a better path. You may discover a stumbling block that you had not seen before. The next Y decision may involve resting on your laurels (the horse's way) or trying a different way—the rider's choice.
Stabilize: persist and overlearn coping skills until they are automatic.	In a world in which most people tend to look for easy ways, the idea of repeated practice may lack appeal. But there is no easy way to unravel and halt procrastination other than to keep working at building tolerance for discomfort and the necessary follow-through competencies that can give you an edge in a world in which procrastination is common. This represents another Y choice: to apply what you know to other areas where procrastination threatens your productive interests. Keep practicing until you have overlearned counter-procrastination principles and pro-efficiency actions. Then, keep practicing.

- *Talk to yourself as though you were your own critic or a person who can calmly and caringly reframe the situation.* An honest reframing may include this perspective: "I don't want to, but I had better act responsibly if I want to avoid a last-minute rush and risk a negative performance review." Sometimes telling yourself that following through is the responsible thing to do can cause a radical shift in perception from avoidance to productive actions.
- *Examine where you feel the discomfort.* Is it in your shoulders? Is it in your stomach? Does stress give you a headache? Does

TABLE 3.2

Your Personal PURRRRS Plan

Procrastination problem: _____.

PURRRRS	Choices Made and Actions Taken
Pause: tune in to what is happening.	
Use cognitive, emotional, and behavioral resources to resist impulses.	
Reflect: think about what is happening.	
Reason and plan out your actions.	
Respond by putting your plan into action.	
Review and revise: make adjustments to improve the plan and the results. When warranted, try another way.	
Stabilize: persist and overlearn coping skills until they are automatic.	

tension seem general? Without engaging in any diversions, is it possible for you to time how long the discomfort lasts? You may find that a measured time shows that tension is relatively brief. There is a biological reason for this: stress from adrenaline has a limited life. So, why run from something limited?

- *Is it possible for you to start something that you feel tempted to put off?* Once you start, do your feelings change? Can you

END PROCRASTINATION NOW! TIP
EMOTION

Energize your prosperity drives by keeping a positive focus.

Move yourself forward toward productive outcomes.

Operate to keep your perspective on long-term advantages.

Tolerate—but don't give in to unpleasant emotions that reflect a false signal for delay.

Integrate realistic thinking with self-regulated actions to support your stated objectives.

Overcome diversionary urges through exercising your PURRRRS choice.

Nudge yourself in the direction of rider Y decisions that promote productive results and aid in the development of emotional muscle.

find added benefits from grabbing the reins and guiding the horse? For example, positive affect increases as goal-directed behavior increases, and vice versa.

- *Think about whether or not you fear discomfort.* Is the anticipation of discomfort enough for you to find a diversion alluring? These discomfort fears are common but manageable. I will show you how to overcome distress as it relates to procrastination in the next chapter.

Help Your Horse Get Past Procrastination-Related Distress

Discomfort-dodging patterns increase the risk that you'll procrastinate again in similar circumstances. Changing the pattern involves developing tolerance for tension. This is a conscious act. When you allow yourself to experience tension, you productively help yourself shift your attention from a procrastination retreat to a forward momentum. If you are not anxious about performance-connected tensions, and you are willing to allow yourself to feel uncomfortable, then you are more likely to follow a positive direction.

Secondary distress is intolerance for tension; you think you can't stand emotions such as fear, anxiety, depression, stress, and feeling overwhelmed. Thus, you have a fear of fear, get depressed over feeling depressed, and feel anxious about feeling anxious—I like to call this phenomenon "double troubles."

Double troubles say more about what you think about yourself than about what you think about a delayed task. Powerless thinking is a common double trouble. If you think you are powerless to deal with negative emotions and procrastination, powerless thinking can layer an added sense of anxiety and vulnerability over an already challenging situation. However, if you thought you could contain and control unpleasant emotions, thoughts about these unpleasant feelings would reflect this tolerance.

Learning to tolerate tension can defuse fear of feelings. If you don't fear tension, then you are less likely to experience tension as a trigger for procrastination. Building emotional muscle and flexing that muscle can have a profound impact on dispatching a double trouble that can be significantly worse than the original tension. Here are a few tips:

- You can start with a question: why can't I stand what I don't like?
- Watch out for Catch-22 procrastination thinking, such as, "I can't change." Respond with a question: where is the evidence that change is impossible?
- Beware of developing an inner voice that encourages you to give in to unhealthy urges, telling you to go ahead and have that extra piece of cake—you deserve it; or you don't have to work today—now is a better time to play. Use your long- and short-term procrastination analysis grid to put this kind of short-term thinking into a rational perspective, and to resist harmful urges.

Double troubles bring you into the realm of cyclical thinking. For example, if you're stuck with Catch-22 procrastination thinking ("I can't change"), look carefully and you can see the cycle: I can't change, and because I can't change, I'll be stressed and procrastinate forever. Take out one element in the circle and define it as an assumption, and you've taken a step toward breaking the circle. Assumptions are not the same as facts!

In this chapter, you saw how to build your emotional muscle when it comes to procrastination. As long as the procrastination lure glistens by increasing your ability to withstand various emotional procrastination traps, you're likely to resist following the lure.

End Procrastination Now! Your Plan

Knowledge without know-how is like living in an ivory tower. Know-how is the collection of skills that you've learned that you apply to produce a productive outcome. Know-how is what brings home the bacon. Harnessing emotional knowledge is a big part of this know-how.

What three ideas for dealing effectively with procrastination have you had? Write them down.

1.

2.

3.

What three top actions can you take to shift from procrastination toward productive actions? Write them down.

1.

2.

3.

What three things did you do to execute your action plan? Write them down.

1.

2.

3.

What did you learn from applying the ideas and action plan that you can use in other areas? Write this down.

1.

2.

3.

4

How to Handle Stress-Related Procrastination

You can't avoid stress—it occurs in every facet of your life. Any major change, such as the birth of a child, taking on new responsibilities, or retirement, can disrupt your equilibrium. Stress is a general term that can be more specifically defined as being frazzled, pressured, nervous, anxious, worried, strained, or tense. Stress is a by-product of your perception of situations and of believing you are short on resources to emotionally cope with a situation. The three-pronged cognitive, emotive, and behavioral approach directly applies to addressing stress and to reducing your use of it as a catalyst for procrastination.

What happens to your body when you feel stressed? Your brain engages your autonomic nervous system (ANS), which involuntarily releases the stress hormones adrenaline and cortisol. When the challenge passes, the body returns to balance (allostasis). However, with excessive stress, your hormones no longer protect the body, but instead rip away at it. Persistent stress is costly to your health. Stress elevates your blood sugar, eventually putting you at risk for type 2 diabetes. When persistent stress routinely disrupts your sleep, this limits your body's ability to restore itself, compromising your immune system; poor sleep patterns can occur and lead to depression.

If you become helpless when coping with stressors, you begin to feel as if you are living in an emotional war zone. Poor coping skills add to an elevated allostatic load. By using cognitive behavioral stress management methods, you can reduce cortisol from chronic fatigue, generalized anxiety, and other stress conditions.

Types of Stress That Can Lead to Procrastination

One of the most common forms of stress is workplace stress, which may have as much to do with adversity as with change. Job satisfaction is declining, with 49 percent of people surveyed indicating that they are less satisfied with their jobs. However, while job satisfaction is desirable, work is for pay and rarely for play. But job stress may have more significant implications than job satisfaction.

You won't find much scientific literature on the connection between procrastination, job stress, job burnout, and low job satisfaction. Does that mean that stress and procrastination are unrelated in the workplace?

If you fear confrontation, you are likely to put off addressing a discussion where you expect disagreement. If you feel uncomfortable about a work function, you are likely to experience an urge to diverge. Does blame avoidance procrastination disappear when you have a choice between taking a risk and playing it safe? Are you likely to put off decisions?

Your positive work reflections can promote feelings of wellbeing that can spread to your leisure time. Your off-hours reflections on the positive aspects of your work can lead to proactive work effort. However, when work is stressful, dealing with stress effectively can give you something positive to think about regarding your coping competencies. I'll walk you through some paces on dealing with job stress procrastination. However, since stress crisscrosses practically every avenue of life, what you learn here has broader implications for leading a life where you feel more in command of yourself and of the controllable events that take place around you,

Working in an environment where layoffs are taking place can feel stressful. However, not everyone is affected in the same way, and you may roll with the punches of life in some situations better than in others. That doesn't mean that stress conditions won't affect how you think, how you feel, and what you do. However, comparatively, you are less affected.

You may be challenged to develop inner freedom under persistently stressful conditions, such as working with difficult coworkers and supervisors, where you are difficult with yourself, and where you find work balance inequities. However, these conditions can be like a fan blowing cold air in your direction. You can turn the fan away from you, and it continues to blow. The wind may blow, and you need not amplify your stress or procrastinate because that happens.

Stress Caused by Others

You are surrounded by a cast of difficult characters, both at work and in other areas of your life—often, you'll find that your relationships with these people slow your ability to meet your goals or do your job. You have names for each. You call one *Joe the Deflector*. Whatever goes wrong gets deflected back to you. The *fabulous faker* looks busy, busy, busy, but you are the one who has to pick up the slack following this faffing procrastination. *Old tried and true* has a familiar mantra: it was good enough for grandfather and it's good enough for him. *One-upmanship* waits for opportunities to make you look bad. *The complainer* draws you in with horror stories about not getting a corner office and having an assigned parking space at a distance from the entryway.

You may get drawn into other people's procrastination intrigues, but you don't have to slip on this slope. Can you cause others to stop diversionary activities so that you don't get diverted from your functions? You might be persuasive and make some gains in that way. However, the person that you have the best chance of controlling is yourself, and imperfectly so. But accepting and letting go of a need to control uncontrollable situations can lead to stress reduction, even under the most adverse work conditions.

Can you accomplish this emotional muscle building under the most extreme stress conditions? Imprisoned in several Nazi concentration camps, psychiatrist Viktor Frankl learned from the ancient Stoic philosophers that he had the freedom to choose his inner thoughts. From the German philosopher Friedrich Nietzsche, he learned that by having a *why* for living, you can bear almost any *how*. His *why* was surviving for his family. If you are engaged with difficult coworkers, family members, or friends, is it possible for you to find purpose and meaning that can help you strip away any added stress you may experience?

In most ongoing adverse situations, I find that people give themselves double trouble. The first is stress from the adversity, and the second is often worse: a fear of the feeling of stress that can amplify the tension. The concept of acceptance that we discussed earlier can have a calming effect: the situation is what it is, stress is what it is, now let me see what I can do to create a more favorable external and internal environment to lessen the stresses.

In many work environments, time is lost due to internal politics, intrigues, and acts of antagonistic cooperation. Lamenting these events and distracting yourself by focusing on them is analogous to getting hit by a bus driver and blaming the driver and cursing the situation. Here is an alternative view about this form of stress: Is it better to curse the driver or rehabilitate yourself so you are no longer afflicted? In the next chapter, I'll describe approaches for taking charge of yourself under adverse conditions where procrastination is especially risky.

END PROCRASTINATION NOW! TIP
Seven Steps to Freeing Yourself from Stress-Related Procrastination

The following seven-step process maps a way to control what you do and advance while others engage in procrastination activities:

1. Identify a clear purpose, a goal, and an organized approach to achieve that goal. You've set a leadership direction for yourself that can translate into conscientious, productive actions.
2. An effective person who can pull together a voluntary group for a common cause sets the tone by getting up front, taking responsibility, and displaying intelligence and capability.
3. Keep focused on your prime objective, act with a strategic mind, make an effort to look for and act on opportunities that will pass unobserved by most, and ask what's missing from the picture.
4. In fluidly changing circumstances, give structure and definition to emerging processes. Keep on top of new developments. Act to take advantage of changing information. Coordinate your resources.
5. The collective intelligence of a group is a rich information resource. Encourage communication. Listen. Judge which people you can count on. However, reserve the final decision for yourself when you have this discretion.
6. In activities where you are in charge, reserve the final decision as your prerogative. Rendering reasoned judgments to gain ground is important.
7. Push distractions aside as quickly as possible. There isn't time for them. Timing, pacing, and maintaining momentum are normally of greater importance.

Self-Inflicted Stress

Most people amplify their own stress problems. You can have a great employer, supportive coworkers, and challenging responsibilities that are comfortably within your capabilities. Still, you carry your work home and fret over what went wrong and what could go wrong tomorrow.

Negative thinking about your goals can affect the quality of your efforts. Connie, a procrastination workshop participant, complained that everyone at her office hated her. That was why she dragged her feet. I asked her how many people worked in her department. She said, 29. I asked for their first names. I then went down the list and asked her to tell me how she knew that each person hated her. This is what it boiled down to: she had sound evidence that a clique of three disliked her. She regularly socialized with six coworkers. The others showed some cordiality. The question is: if everyone hates you, how do you explain the exceptions? Once Connie got past her misperception, she began to act cooperatively, and she reported feeling better about her work. When she started thinking less about imaginary problems, Connie reported that she procrastinated less. There are numerous potential stressors around you. If establishing control decreases stress, can you establish inner control and direction to survive falling into procrastination traps?

Anxiety and Complex Procrastination

Procrastination increases with worry, anxiety, and depression. These complex procrastination catalysts are common.

As you may recall from Chapter 1, complex procrastination is a combination of procrastination plus a coexisting condition, such as anxiety, self-doubt, or low tension tolerance. Complex procrastination delays include delaying the task and putting off dealing with the complex co-occurring condition that contributes to procrastination. Let's suppose that you want to convey unpleasant information to a coworker about how the person's delays are impeding a project. You delay because you have a confrontation anxiety. You believe that if you assert your interests, this will lead to an unpleasant verbal encounter that you tell yourself you'll lose. By ending procrastination caused by your confrontation anxiety, you may persuade the coworker to follow through in a timely way. Thus, you have a double gain.

A procrastination habit that co-occurs with self-doubts is a common situation. Here, procrastination can be both a symptom and a cause. You put off a timely and relevant activity. You experience an ongoing nagging anxiety about the incomplete task. You continue to think that you can't cope with the complexity of the activity. This adds to your uncertainty about performing effectively. This self-doubt is a double jeopardy. It can both trigger procrastination and result from procrastination.

A self-doubt state of mind rarely occurs without other co-occurring conditions that also lead to procrastination. Self-doubts, perfectionism, fear of disapproval, fear of failure, and fear of tension are part of the procrastination evaluative style cluster where you have multiple coexisting problem conditions, but one *evaluation* theme and some branch issues to address.

Let's take a look at an evaluation procrastination cluster, shown in Table 4.1. I'll briefly describe what distinguishes each aspect and give a conceptual direction to overcome procrastination.

When you boil down related cluster conditions into a core theme, you may find complex clusters less imposing. As you engage in productive activities to progress on those activities and cut back on evaluative anxieties, you can shorten your learning curve for addressing and overcoming this form of complex procrastination.

Committed, Positive, and Proactive Coping

When you modulate, you adjust a tone or volume to change a signal. Let's look at the language of commitment and challenge as

TABLE 4.1

Evaluation Procrastination Cluster

Cluster Evaluation Dimension	Conceptual Direction
Self-doubt. Practically everyone has periods of insecurity. Self-doubt patterns are different. You view yourself as lacking adequate resources and abilities and needing certainty. Thus, you are likely to second-guess yourself, hesitate, doubt yourself, and procrastinate in areas where you are not sure that you'll perform adequately. Facing areas of uncertainty is likely to evoke anxiety and create more hesitations and doubts. You evaluate yourself as lacking resources and unable to perform well enough.	1. If you fall into the self-doubt trap, consider taking a pluralistic view of yourself. This pluralistic view balances the tunnel vision signature of self-doubts. You have hundreds of traits, qualities, and emotions and the potential to do well in multiple ways. It's important that you take stock of a pluralistic you and what you are truly able to do. 2. Doubts grow from uncertainties. Uncertainties are part of life. Without them, human growth and development would be limited. I don't know how anyone can avoid uncertainty. 3. Hesitations and self-downing suggest that you can benefit from peeling off a layer of the onion and looking to see whether your self-evaluations have anything to do with a perfectionist view.
Perfectionism. You may think of a perfectionist as an insecure, hostile, achievement-driven, time-urgent, Type A personality. That description appears overly general. If you set impossibly high standards, think in terms of polar opposites (winner-loser), assert entitlement, and make your worth contingent on meeting lofty standards, you may drive yourself to avoid failure or engage in self-handicapping to justify procrastination. You can be paralyzed by worrying about imperfections and expend energy detecting defects. If you believe that you can't be what you should be, you've fallen into an evaluation trap.	1. If you fall into the Type A perfectionist trap, take a second look. With your focus on activity, what are the critical areas in your life that repeatedly get put on the back burner? How do you judge or evaluate your ability to participate in those areas? 2. If you fall into a challenge avoidance perfectionist trap because you expect more from yourself than you can deliver, you are running against the grain of reality. Life is as it is. It is not globally as you think it should be. 3. Entitlement claims exist in the mind. Judging reality against these expectations leads to a false evaluation of what you and others should do. Instead of prejudging, work to suspend perfectionist judgment. Take a pluralistic perspective where "gray" is the norm. Test what you can do, rather than stretching for something that you cannot reach.

TABLE 4.1 (continued)

Cluster Evaluation Dimension	Conceptual Direction
Fear of disapproval. If you believe that your worth depends on the approval of others, you may undertake a quixotic mission to be a universal people pleaser. You may emphasize what others want of you and fall behind on your own personal responsibilities, or you may avoid purposeful and productive actions for fear that you'll step on someone's toes and get judged. Evaluation comes into play when you worry too much about what other people think, and especially when you think that others think that you've fallen short.	1. The ability to get along with others is a traditional social standard for success. However, you can't win them all. No reasonable person would expect that of you. 2. In keeping with the cluster evaluation theme, think about the concept of obligatory perfectionism. Here you obligate yourself to please and to not disappoint others. Obligatory perfectionism can lead to procrastination when you bite off more than you can chew, or when you resent the obligation. 3. The pluralistic view comes into play in yet another corrective way. Since both you and others are likely to have varied interests, desires, values, and tastes, what productive directions are available through taking a pluralistic view?
Fear of failure. Like other parts of the cluster, this fear involves evaluation: how you evaluate yourself, and beliefs about other's evaluations and what they say about you and your value. Fear of success is often the second side of the coin. If you succeed, perhaps you will later fail; people may expect more from you, and you won't be able to deliver.	1. If you fear failure, what is the failure that you fear? How do you define it? What are the examples? Who gives out the report card? 2. Most problems that you'll face are like experiments in living. Some responses are likely to be more productive than others, and some may be different, but still useful. 3. The option of evaluating what you do in a pluralistic, changing world is reasonable, but globally evaluating yourself in any permanent way based upon how well you do in any one situation is not realistic. 4. As for fear of success, you first have to succeed to see if there is anything to fear later. In a fixed and predictable world, there is no guarantee that you'll fail after succeeding, or that more than you can handle will be expected from you.

procrastination modulators. Then, we'll look at proactive coping to boost your do-it-now signals to promote productive outcomes.

Using Commitment Language

American diplomat and scientist Ben Franklin advised committing only to what you are willing to do, then doing it. A commitment is a pledge or a promise to yourself or to someone else that you'll follow through on a responsibility now or at a future time. You may have competing commitments, such as saving for a new home, having the money to enjoy life, and investing for retirement. Such competing commitments suggest that one thing or another is going to get put off.

You may commit to losing weight, improving the quality of your work products, and ending procrastination practices. However, without a plan and an intention, this is like a promissory note with no due date. If you delay, you're on the slippery procrastination slope.

If you choose to stay off the slippery slope, before you voluntarily make a commitment, ask yourself: What am I doing this for? (It's easy to skip this step.) A few more preliminary questions are in order: What do you want to accomplish? What is required? What resources do you need? How long do you expect the process to take? What are the constraints? Now you may be ready to commit to an action of your choice.

A phrase as simple as "I will do this" is a commitment. The stronger your sense of intent, the more likely it is that you'll follow through. However, you're not off the procrastination slope until you start acting with purpose and intent.

Organizations that live up to their commitments to produce high-quality products and deliver better-than-average customer service are likely to keep their customers and add to their customer base. View yourself as your own best customer. What service do you believe you deserve from yourself?

Using Positive Challenge Language

Psychologist James Blascovich found that if you believe you have the resources to meet or exceed the demands of a situation, you will feel challenged. In a challenge state, you are likely to feel excited about meeting the challenge and overcoming the obstacles. This positive *challenge stress* promotes cardiac efficiency and mental agility.

Perceptions of threat have the opposite effect. If you believe that you don't have what it takes to meet a challenge, you are likely to feel threatened. Threat decreases your efficiency and mental agility. This state of mind also increases your chances of procrastinating.

Threat perceptions are part of a process of coming to a conclusion about whether it's worth taking the initiative to follow through. However, perceptions are often filtered through beliefs. *Threat stresses* commonly arise from irrational worries, resentments, and negative thoughts, such as, "I don't have what it takes." "I'll be embarrassed." "I'll look like a fool." This language of threat portends a psychic danger, and this danger is a red-carpet invitation to procrastination.

A shift from threat to challenge language can pull the red carpet out from under procrastination. The language of challenge involves using action terms to structure a positive process of moving from procrastination threat thinking to challenge thinking and follow-up actions. When you use challenge language, you give yourself directions for taking specific concrete steps toward constructive goals. This is a conscious assertion and direction, as you see in the following example:

This is my goal or opportunity: _____.
This is what I'm prepared to do: _____.
This is when I'll start: _____.

This is how I'll benefit: _____.

This is how I'll persist: _____.

Challenge language thinking has nothing to do with inspirational statements, such as, "You can do it. You'll succeed." If platitudes and slogans were effective, we'd all use them, and there would be no procrastination.

Proactive Coping to Meet Positive Challenges

When you proactively cope, you prepare yourself to meet challenges before they occur. This proactive approach helps prevent last-minute procrastination rushes and can promote a low-stress and high-productivity approach to meeting work challenges.

Is proactive coping a new idea? Hardly. It's been part of the organizational lexicon for generations. However, the label and the process invite research initiatives. The preliminary results are encouraging. This forward-looking approach to managing goals (challenge outlook) appears to be effective in promoting positive results and less stress. Positive striving through taking proactive steps appears to be associated with a sense of well-being.

When you proactively cope, you appraise the situation using the information you have available. To fill gaps, you research key points. You figure out what you can accomplish. This self-regulatory format is used for addressing challenges before they become stressful.

You are scheduled for a problem-solving meeting on how to maintain ongoing performance review records and increase their accuracy and value. You're nervous about the meeting. Your usual procrastination decision is to think that you'll get to this planning stage later. Then you let time run until immediately before the meeting and rush to finish.

Keeping on top of performance review information is appealing. You don't relish the thought of a flurry of last-minute effort to get performance reviews done, using the last two weeks or so for a reference. Facing subordinates with incomplete information is an added strain. So, how do you proactively cope under such circumstances?

Your proactive coping goal for the meeting is to act proactively. You'll take a look at the issue and prepare a position. You'll research the area and distill your findings into a position. You may not precisely know your position before you start. That is the purpose of proactively doing the research.

END PROCRASTINATION NOW! TIP
Four Steps to Proactive Coping

Step 1: Accept ambiguity and uncertainty as normal for upcoming situations. You help yourself reduce fears of uncertainty through exercising your proactive coping resources. You won't see the complete picture until you engage the challenge; the more knowledge you develop, the more gaps you can discover. That is typically better than relying on an illusion that the future will be better without your making any effort today.

Step 2: Think about potential stumbling blocks that can predictably get in the way, such as stress thinking. Plan to proactively cope with this and other expected impediments in advance of their occurrence.

Step 3: Prepare and gather information to create a plan that you can modify with new information. As you actively engage in this constructive process, you can build momentum for other preparatory steps further down the line.

Step 4: Actively work to develop a time perspective for proactive coping, or the process may get caught up in the same time vortex as other delayed activities. A commitment about when you'll start and what you'll do first can start the process in motion and make the difference. Apply challenge language about how, when, and where you'll proactively cope.

When you arrive at the meeting, you are unlikely to have all the answers. The purpose of the meeting is to flesh out the issues and come to reasoned conclusions. However, when you are prepared, you are likely to see the meeting as a challenge. You don't feel the usual stress and strain where you hope to go unnoticed in the meeting.

Curbing Low-Frustration-Tolerance Procrastination

Low frustration tolerance is a strong aversion for tension that can lead to discomfort dodging and procrastination. This sensitivity to unpleasant sensations gets worse when it is magnified by self-talk, such as, "The task is too tough, and I can't stand doing it." These tension-amplifying thoughts are a slippery slope to procrastination practices. Questions such as what makes the task too tough and why you can't stand what you don't like can expose the false evaluative dimension of this thinking.

Building high frustration tolerance is a significant life challenge. If you don't fear or avoid tension, you are likely to feel that you are in command of yourself and of the controllable events that take place around you. Paradoxically, you are also less likely to experience amplified tensions when you don't fear them. With high frustration tolerance, you are likely to take on more challenges and experience more accomplishment and satisfaction from the actions that you undertake. Building and using counter-procrastination skills helps decrease tension fears as you boost your self-efficacy skills.

Tension avoidance through procrastination practically always involves an evaluation. Exaggerated evaluations about discomfort tend to lead to discomfort dodging. The evaluations that lead to discomfort dodging tend to interact with self-doubts and increase vulnerability to procrastination. If you reduce either your self-doubts or your intolerance for tension, you've acted to reduce both conditions along with weakening a co-occurring procrastination habit.

Build Stress Buffers against Low Frustration Tolerance

Frustration-tolerance training can be counted among the most powerful ways to reduce both stress and procrastination that is associated with stress and that sets conditions for added stress. Here are three broad directions:

1. *Build your body* to buffer pressures from multiple ongoing frustrations. Ongoing stress increases the risk of disease, fatigue, and mood disorders, and so building your body has an added value in reducing these risks. Build this buffer through regular exercise; a healthy diet; maintaining a reasonable weight for your gender, height, and age; and getting adequate sleep.
2. *Liberate your mind from ongoing stress thinking.* This includes dealing with pessimistic and perfectionist thinking as well as low-frustration-tolerance self-talk, such as telling yourself something like, "I can't take this; I have to have relief right now."
3. Change patterns that you associate with needless frustration, such as holding back on going after what you want, avoiding contention at all costs, and inhibiting yourself from engaging in the normal pursuits of happiness and from actions to curb procrastination.

(For more information on frustration-tolerance development, I've provided a free e-book. To access the book, visit http://www.rebtnetwork.org/library/How_to_Conquer_Your_Frustrations.pdf.)

The Importance of Maintaining Optimal Performance Tensions

Since stress is inevitable, why not accept this reality and figure out how to make stress work for you? The Yerkes-Dodson curve shows the proven relationship between arousal and performance that you can use to put threat and challenge into a visual perspective while adding an undermotivated dimension (see Figure 4.1).

The slope at the extreme left of the curve shows low arousal and motivation. The slope at the extreme right shows the effects of negative thinking. The region between the two dots in the middle shows an optimal range of arousal. However, some productive activities involve different levels of arousal. Answering a phone and finishing a Masters in Business Administration degree take different levels of arousal. However, the curve is quite okay as an awareness tool for putting arousal into perspective.

If you have a low arousal level for a high-priority activity, your challenge is to either push yourself to start and finish or find an incentive. Pushing yourself is a form of arousal. A possible motivating incentive is to get an unwanted task off your back.

If your mind is filled with threat stress thoughts, you'll probably have trouble solving a complex problem. When tension is at the extreme, it can be so distracting and disorganizing that you seem to have little time and energy to do anything else. The challenge is to "take a breather," such as a walk around the block. Plan to shift to a self-observant perspective, perhaps by recording and

FIGURE 4.1
The Yerkes-Dodson Curve

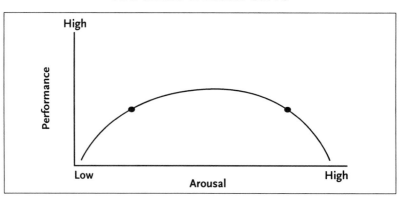

END PROCRASTINATION NOW! TIP
The POWER Plan

Proactively cope with upcoming challenges by setting a design for achievement.

Outline a commitment and challenge thinking approach to support proactive coping.

Work to execute a coping program to operate productively and reduce stress.

Evaluate your progress and not yourself.

Repeat this proactive challenge and commitment thinking approach until it feels natural.

organizing what is going on using the ABCDE problem-solving format. This organization initiative actively sets the stage for engaging the problem with a clearer, calmer, mind and a directed sense of purpose.

The curve serves as a reminder of the benefits of challenge arousal and that this arousal is healthy. Indeed, much learning and remembering is motivated by adaptive forms of tension.

Breaking the procrastination habit takes work, and this is best done by working at what you put off. There is another dimension to this: when procrastination is a symptom of distressing thinking, the most direct line to freedom is to follow through without diversion; evaluate this thinking using Socrates', Frankl's, and Ellis's prescriptions. If these ways aren't successful, try another.

End Procrastination Now! Your Plan

You can learn to buffer yourself against stress conditions that coexist with procrastination conditions such as anxiety, catastrophizing, and feeling overwhelmed. What will work best for you?

What three ideas have you had that you can use to help yourself deal with procrastination behaviors effectively? Write them down.

1.

2.

3.

What is your action plan? What are the three top actions you can take to promote purposeful and productive outcomes? Write them down.

1.

2.

3.

What implementation actions did you take? Write them down.

1.

2.

3.

What three things did you learn from applying the ideas and the action plan, and how can you next use this information? Write them down.

1.

2.

3.

The Behavioral Approach:
Follow Through to Get It Done

5

Act Decisively

A conscious decision to act decisively is the first step in initiating behavioral follow-through. Once you've become aware of triggers that cause habitual procrastination, you've emotionally coped with the unpleasant task, you've made an active decision to get the task done, and you actively follow through, then you've stopped your procrastination cycle. Overcoming indecision is a key part of this positive change process, and you'll learn how to get off the fence and follow through with what is important for you to do.

The fourth-century Chinese general Sun Tzu stated that if you know your enemy and yourself, there is no need to fear the results of 100 battles. Sun Tzu's statement refers to decision making as well as to war. If you know why you put off major decisions, know how to make reasoned ones that work for you, and then persist in following through, you've ended procrastination. That won't happen 100 percent of the time, any more than winning all battles is a realistic option. However, you can load the dice in your favor, and you can learn to do that here.

Decision making is an ongoing part of being human. What makes for a good decision? How do you get to that point? Unfortunately, there are no guaranteed guidelines on how to make decisions. Decision-making situations vary widely. Different situations may require you to apply different values, rules, or procedures. Some decisions involve resolving conflicts. Others contain opportunities, but also risks and uncertainties. The options you face can include tough choices. You may have unwanted trade-offs and lesser-of-evils choices. You may experience conflict between giving up a great opportunity that's out of reach and choosing one that is attainable, but of lesser value. An ideology or bias can influence the direction of the decision unfavorably. Knowing yourself, then, is important in decision making.

How do you improve the quality and timeliness of your decisions when procrastination interferes? In this two-stage process, you learn to get out of a decision-making procrastination holding pattern and act to make and execute purposeful and productive decisions.

To advance this two-stage process, I organized this chapter into three parts. The first describes factors that are involved in indecision. The second is about ending decision-making procrastination. The third discusses how to make and carry out productive decisions.

Procrastination, Uncertainty, and Indecision

The Latin word *decido* is the root of *decision*. It has two meanings: to decide, and also to fall off. To avoid a fall, you may decide not to decide. However, if you've adopted the no-failure plan from earlier in this book, and you emphasize discovery over blame avoidance, "falling" like an autumn leave is not an option.

In this section, let's look at uncertainty as a condition for indecisiveness. It discusses four ways to overcome decision-making procrastination, avoid needless pain from sitting on a spiked fence, and act to secure useful gains.

In ambiguous situations you don't see the full picture. You are aware that you face unknowns. You have no guarantee of success regardless of what you do. When you feel unsure and doubtful, you may avoid making a decision even when managing the uncertainty is a pressing priority.

Uncertainty may stimulate doubts, challenge, or something in between. However, is a high-priority situation with unknowns automatically a cause for stress and procrastination? It depends on how you define the situation and your tolerance for uncertainty.

If you are among the millions who are intolerant of uncertainty, you may find this intolerance rooted in a highly evaluative process. For example, oversensitivity to discomfort plus either exaggerating and dramatizing the dreadfulness of the situation or seeing it as being as bad as, if not worse than, it can possibly be amplifies the tension. Under these amplified stress conditions, it is understandable that a procrastination path of least resistance can seem appealing.

Let's look at four conditions associated with intolerance for uncertainty and procrastination: illusions, heuristics, worry, and equivocation.

Illusion-Based Decisions

Your intuition, insightfulness, and emotional sensitivity were present before your reason developed. The evolution of reason and foresight opened opportunities to go beyond survival to higher-level choices and decisions. However, a tool that is an asset can also be a liability.

A psychological illusion is a blend of intuition and false thinking. It is something that you believe is real and true, but that in fact isn't the way you perceive or read it. Psychological illusions can and do arise as answers for reducing uncertainty.

Do you believe that you make illusion-based decisions that can give you a false sense of clarity, but also a high decision error rate? Few people believe that illusions have a controlling influence over their lives. But illusions often interfere with identifying rational choices and deciding on what to do to best meet the challenge.

You probably have illusion hot spots that coexist with procrastination. Indeed, procrastination sometimes reflects the mind-fogging power of illusion. The tomorrow or mañana belief is an illusion of false hope. Believing that you can't manage uncertainty can map into an illusion of inferiority. If you do not see your harmful psychological illusions, you are likely to repeat self-defeating patterns without knowing why.

If you act as though you think your assumptions are the same as facts, you may operate with an *illusion of understanding*. You can misread situations with confidence and make decisions based on this misreading. Harvard economist John Kenneth Galbraith noted that when people are the least sure, they tend to be the most dogmatic.

Here is a sample of illusions that taint decision making:

- *Illusion of judgment.* You believe that your judgments are invariably accurate. However, for this to be true, you would have to have the best of all authoritative information and be entirely objective and free from bias.
- *Illusion of emotional insight.* You assume that if you feel strongly about something, you must be right. Based on this supposed emotional insight, you are likely to judge on the basis of your first emotional impressions with very little else to go on.
- *Illusion of superiority.* You assume that you are smarter and more capable than anyone else. Thus, you automatically reject suggestions or alternative courses of action that are inconsistent with your own views.
- *Illusion of inferiority.* You underestimate your capabilities even when your actions show greater capabilities. When you limit yourself in order to maintain consistency with this view of yourself, you risk making it a self-fulfilling prophecy.

Here is a brief proactive coping exercise for addressing psychological illusions, making realistic decisions, and avoiding procrastinating on decision making.

Awareness: You can recognize an illusion by its results. If you believe that you need to make perfect decisions, you'll lose opportunity after opportunity. Lost opportunity is a result.	Action: Flip things around and try to disconfirm the psychological illusions that come across your awareness screen. For example, ask yourself, "Where is the uncontestable evidence that the decision I am tempted to make is fact-based? What are the facts that support the decision?"

Overreliance on Heuristics

In an unfamiliar situation, you may rely on heuristics, or examples, to guide your decisions. These rules of thumb, common sense, or selected tidbits or examples from experience take many forms. "When in doubt, flip a coin" is a heuristic.

Heuristics can map a path to better planning and decision making. You may profitably use a heuristic of mentally working back from a future time when you've achieved a goal. By reflecting on the steps you took, you may help yourself get past a planning bottleneck.

When there are gaps in your knowledge and you have virtually no time to study an issue, trusting your feelings may be the best thing to do. If something doesn't feel right, it may not be right. You're offered a deal that you have to decide on right away. It sounds too good to be true. You rely on emotional cues and past experience to assess the offer. You pass on the deal. However, some heuristics have a downside in that they lead to poor decisions, and some hide procrastination.

- *Heuristics sometimes work well enough.* However, rules of thumb can lead to distortions and bad decisions. You believe that someone who looks you straight in the eye is honest, but here is a paradox: pathological liars will normally look straight at you, whereas a shy but unusually honest person may avoid eye contact.

- *The fundamental attribution error is among the best-validated heuristics.* This is the tendency to see your own errors as situational and explainable. When observing the errors of others, however, you do the opposite: you downplay situational factors and attribute poor results to character flaws, such as "laziness." This is part of a tendency to understand your own situation and exonerate yourself from blame, and then blame the other guy for actions that you wouldn't blame yourself for if you were the actor. *If you rely heavily on "gut" impressions, your decisions are likely to be arbitrary and biased.* Saying that you rely on gut impressions is often a cover for *expediency procrastination.* When you rely on gut impressions, you don't have to prepare and make a studied decision. Thus, relying on gut feelings can be unwise.

Heuristics are normally more efficient than the automatic reactions of perception, where a whisper of negative emotion is sufficient to trigger a procrastination sequence. However, because heuristics are blanket rules, they are normally inferior to a reasoned-out assessment. Here is a brief proactive coping approach for improving heuristic-biased decision making by adding some reflective components.

Awareness: Separate perceptual reactions from heuristics from reflective preparation. By doing so, you'll know where you stand in decision-making situations.	*Action*: Decide which of the different decision-making responses is appropriate for the situation. Does the urge to diverge fit with your longer-term objectives? Are the heuristics in this case free from realty-distorting bias? What does taking a studied approach offer?

Worry and Procrastination

When you worry, you show intolerance for uncertainty. You fill in the gaps with assumptions about harmful possibilities. You tense yourself over threatening and catastrophic possibilities that you have no knowledge of actually happening.

This cognitive and emotional distraction may prompt procrastination.

Worry and procrastination share certain features. Both have a specious reward. When the catastrophic possibility doesn't happen, you feel relieved. Relief is a reward for a worry where the dreaded results don't happen. A decision to act later can feel relieving and rewarding. Relief is a reward when it increases the frequency of the act that it follows, making worry or procrastination, for instance, more likely to recur in similar circumstances.

Here is a brief proactive coping exercise for defusing worry-stimulated procrastination.

Awareness: If you worry too much about making wrong choices, you have a false belief(s) that underpin(s) worry. You may believe that you need certainty under uncertain conditions.	*Action*: Beliefs are convictions, but conviction doesn't make a belief true. To put matters into perspective, think about the best and worst things that can happen and many in-between results. Think about what you'd have to do to achieve each. What is the most probable outcome that you can control?

Perfection and Equivocation

If mulling over pros and cons puts you in a procrastination holding pattern, this equivocation can set the stage for a perfect cognitive, emotive, and behavioral storm for making an impulsive decision. For 15 years, Willow looked for her perfect soul mate. Equivocating over one potential mate after another, she couldn't decide. As a skilled defect detector, she found flaws in everyone, angered herself over their imperfections, and eventually unceremoniously rejected all of them.

Then the time came when Willow's biological clock was winding down. She singled out the issue of having babies, and that became her priority. Finding the perfect soul mate was no longer a priority. Marriage became the means to the end of having children. Tony, who had a serious alcohol addiction, was available. She impulsively married him. Two years and two kids later, an unemployed Tony has refused to stop drinking. Willow has another major decision to make, and she is uncertain what to do.

Here is a brief proactive coping exercise for addressing decision-making equivocation.

Awareness: It can seem as if you are going through an endless loop if you keep going over the same ground and adding conditions and qualifications. Equivocation, then, reflects a need for certainty. However, only the most relevant conditions need to be met.	*Action*: Most decisions that include uncertainties carry a real possibility that the decision will be adequate but imperfect. Occam's razor refers to the idea that conditions should not be needlessly made more complicated than they actually are, and that the simplest explanation is normally the best. Simplify.

Combating Decision-Making Procrastination

An automatic procrastination decision (APD) starts with a primitive perceptional whisper of emotion and an urge to diverge. APDs may come from subconscious causes, such as perceiving something in the situation as complex and unsettling.

A higher-order APD occurs when you make a promissory note to yourself to do later something that you can start now. This can trigger a chain of procrastination thoughts:

"I don't know which action is the most important or where to
    begin. I'll rest on it."
"I need more references."
"I need to read more before I can start."
"I won't be able to start today because there isn't enough time."
"I'll get to it later."

A false *later is better* decision can glide under the radar of reason. When that happens, more procrastination decisions may follow. You decide to coddle yourself by telling yourself, "I'm too tired to think." If your performance is later diminished, you can excuse yourself because you were once fatigued. And when the time comes to decide again, you self-handicap yourself again to sanitize a delay.

Thinking about your thinking and connecting the dots between procrastination thinking and its consequences puts you in a better position to decide on a productive course or action, and this is often a first step in asserting control over the procrastination process.

Contesting Decision-Making Procrastination

APDs are a predictable part of lateness procrastination and other procrastination styles. *Lateness procrastination* is when you dabble with nonessential activities and keep dabbling past the time when you should get going to arrive at a destination. Dabbling, or doing such things as dusting, showering, or making phone calls, is your APD. In *drifting procrastination*, you routinely put off creating life objectives and bind yourself to a sense of purposelessness and APDs such as TV watching. Decision-making procrastination, like lateness and drifting procrastination, is a distinctive procrastination style. It also has APDs, but they occur in the context of avoiding decisions.

Decision-making procrastination is a process of needlessly postponing timely and important decisions until another day and time. You have a choice of relocating to Boston or Miami for your job. Both have roughly equivalent advantages and disadvantages. If you put off the decision until you come up with the perfect answer, you've entered the decision-making procrastination trap.

Let's look at techniques and strategies for ending decision-making procrastination and building decision-making skills. These joint methods include singling out what is important, exercising a do-it-now alternative, following through with a rational decision process, strategic planning, and problem solving.

Singling Out What Is Important to Do

Making a decision based on two or three of the most important factors in a situation is rarely a waste of time. Then when you single out one choice from among others, you've made it the most important. Deciding can be as direct as that.

In a work world with multiple responsibilities and conflicting priorities, how do you know if you are on track with your main priority? You can use the following priority matrix to rank information from what is most pressing and important to your "not important" and "nonpressing" activities. This priority defining matrix approach is a classic type of time management technique that can aid in making decisions about what to emphasize; the most important and pressing activity obviously takes center stage.

ACTION	Important	Useful	Not Important
Pressing			
Nonpressing			

If an activity is important but not pressing, and nothing else is higher on your list, this is an activity that you can start without feeling rushed. For example, you know that you have a distant deadline for consolidating and simplifying 12 different but related production forms into one page of information. Rather than straightening out your files (not important and nonpressing), you attack the consolidation project. You've created an opportunity to get this activity done before it rises to a pressing status. The matrix also helps you distinguish between a priority and a diversion. If you do nonpressing and nonimportant activities over the important and pressing ones, then you can assume that you are procrastinating on the priority.

Exercising the Do-It-Now Choice

Is it the situation or what you make of it that stirs anxiety over uncertainty that can lead to decision-making procrastination? The situation is the stimulus. It is not the cause. Rather, it's both the situation and how you view it that influence what you decide. Your decision may also be affected by what you think about the process of executing the decision and the results you anticipate. These considerations can lead to dancing around a decision or moving directly toward making a choice and following through with action.

Although hesitation in uncertain situations is normal, hesitation plus procrastination suggests a complex form of procrastination. For example, feeling frozen by indecision is a probable symptom of anxiety over uncertainty.

Table 5.1 gives sample decision-making procrastination distractions and sample do-it-now choices.

TABLE 5.1

Decision-Making Procrastination Position	Do-It-Now Choice
Decision procrastination position: You want to play it safe and avoid making a mistake. Your think that errors on your part are awful. So you straddle the fence, awaiting a guarantee before you act.	*Alternative do-it-now choice*: Challenge yourself to put acceptance over indecisiveness assumptions, such as that mistakes are awful. How can you both accept reality as being filled with uncertainties and think that mistakes are awful?
Decision procrastination position: You tell yourself horror stories about real or imagined uncertainties and dramatize the fearsomeness of a situation, leading to your feeling overwhelmed.	*Alternative do-it-now choice*: Gather information that is relevant and make a goodwill effort to decide on an action based upon the available information.

Although there is no sure formula that can guarantee the correctness of a decision before the results are in, inaction caused by indecisiveness is the wrong decision in the vast majority of situations. Act on the 49/51 principle: if you have a slight leaning in one direction, take that direction until the results suggest following a different path. How do you decide the percentages? There is no perfect solution, especially when a decision could go either way. Figure out the pros and cons of each direction, and the picture may begin to clear and give you weight to one direction over another.

Solving Problems and Following Through

What if you don't recognize a decision-making procrastination problem, yet you suffer from the results of indecision? There is not much you can do. A big part of solving a decision-making procrastination problem is to recognize the problem. This can be tricky when different styles of procrastination coexist.

Decision-making procrastination can be cinched by other procrastination styles, such as blame avoidance procrastination, in which you defer a decision to avoid risking criticism. If you tend to follow a behavioral procrastination path, you decide on a direction, establish goals, and generate a strategic plan to meet your objective. Then it comes time for you to execute your plan. You are uncertain what to do when you meet your first barrier. In good behavioral procrastination fashion, you put off following through. When styles interconnect because of, say, uncertainty anxieties, you have the usual two problems to resolve: following through on the counter-procrastination action while addressing the co-occurring condition.

Information from this book can help clarify conditions in which procrastination is a problem condition, and the following problem-solving list covers how to meet this form of challenge:

1. A problem exists when you have a gap between where you are and where you'd like to be. The gap contains unknowns, and solving the problem is ordinarily going to require an evaluation, generating solutions, testing the solutions, and overpowering coexisting procrastination processes when they interfere with preparation for and execution of the solutions.

2. A lot depends on how you define a problem situation. A well-articulated question can help point you in a direction where you can find answers. Directions for solutions are often built into such questions. For example, what steps are involved in ending decision-making procrastination that applies to your situation? This question focuses on the problem and the importance of identifying steps for a solution.

3. Next, define the problem conditions. New questions can stimulate answers that expand and clarify problem-related issues. What, where, when, how, and why questions help to flesh out problem identification issues. *What* pressing decisions are you likely to duck? *Where* is this likely to occur? At what point (*when*) are you most likely to delay? What do you tell yourself when you hesitate? *Why* do you think you find it so troublesome to decide this issue? Play with different scenarios in which you reverse the questions to give direction to acting efficiently and effectively.

4. Reframing problems can lead to different options and conclusions. The idea is to reframe the situation so that you move from a procrastination to a do-it-now track. Use questions to reframe the process. What if my assumptions are inaccurate? What assumptions are likely to be accurate? What other assumptions can I consider? Imagine that your decision leads to unexpected consequences (which can be positive, negative, or both) without putting down or praising yourself. Obtain three alternative views from three people who ordinarily have different perspectives.

In solving a well-articulated problem, you may have many false runs in which you test solutions that don't solve the problem. You may find solutions that are good enough but not perfect. However, once you engage the decision-making process, you are likely to find ways to actualize your capabilities by stretching them.

American diplomat and scientist Ben Franklin stated in his autobiography that by setting goals and striving to reach them, he found that he was not perfect, but he was still far better off than he would have been if he had not undertaken the challenges he set for himself.

Applying a Rational Decision Process

Problem solving may go into a holding pattern when decision-making procrastination gets in the way. Table 5.2 compares a decision breakdown process to a rational decision-making process.

The comparison in the table provides another way to view a Y decision: as a shift from a decision breakdown process to a rational process of making decisions based on concrete realities, where you weigh and balance choices, then act on the best option available at

TABLE 5.2

Decision Breakdown Process	Rational Decision-Making Process
Vague, ambiguous, and unclear problem definition	Clear, concrete, problem statement with measurable and attainable objectives
Reliance on emotion for judgment	Reasoned approach that takes positive values and ethics into account
Self-absorbed focus on avoidance and escape	Self-observant focus on actions to solve the defined problem
Escalating indecisiveness	Accelerating problem-solving actions
Stalling on rendering a decision	Coming to a resolution as a natural extension of the original decision to act

the time. When you face a Y decision between retreating and advancing, use this breakdown-rational contrast. It may be useful to ask who is calling the shots, the horse or the rider?

A Strategic Initiative to Act Decisively

The nineteenth-century Prussian military strategist Carl von Clausewitz's book *On War* has attracted interest from people in the business world who are interested in strategic planning. Its strategic planning content is of value to organizations that want to establish momentum, moving forward in changing circumstances where adaptation is critical. You can apply this same approach to improving the quality of your decisions, getting out of an indecision holding pattern, and enjoying the fruits of your productive labors.

Von Clausewitz's approach centers on strategic planning and execution. He starts by defining strategy as the planning of a campaign that includes the coordination of tactics to achieve the main objective. These tactics are smaller-scale plans to manage each individual encounter. You can apply both strategy and tactics to go against procrastination and to end procrastination.

END PROCRASTINATION NOW! TIP:
DECIDE

Decisions are inescapable, so you might as well decide to decide.

Enter areas of uncertainty to gain clarity and direction.

Consider alternatives and consequences. Include the consequences of inaction.

Implement problem-solving actions.

Determine what works and what doesn't and what could be useful with modifications.

Engage the next challenge and persist in actualizing your positive capabilities.

TABLE 5.3

Von Clausewitz Principles	Counter-Procrastination Applications
1. *Principle of preparation.* A victory is not achieved blindly. A thorough understanding and preparation prior to action are important. Circumstances determine the plan and its usefulness. Decisions are affected by preparations that were made prior to the decision.	*Awareness*: Although emergency situations mandate decisive actions, a well-articulated and well-thought-through plan normally improves the ability to come to a solution. *Action*: Put enough time into preparation to ensure that you have covered as many bases as is reasonable before you start. Test and rate the plan, but not yourself.
2. *Principle of adaptability.* Rules cannot be imposed absolutely in every case; adaptations for special circumstances are necessary. However, similar elements reappear, and this simplifies the planning.	*Awareness*: Procrastination has varied causes and different styles, but also consistent elements, such as diversions into less productive areas. *Action*: Separate similar features from special features and adjust your action to deal with the familiar and special features. Relying on heuristics may be a special feature of decision-making procrastination. Adapt your approach to address these heuristics.
3. *Principle of concentration.* Focus your attention in the direction of importance and avoid dispersing your time and energy. Concentrate your efforts for maximum impact.	*Awareness*: Procrastination is a series of concentrated distraction actions. A radical shift is to concentrate your actions on productive processes and outcomes. *Action*: Challenge yourself to identify an area where you'd ordinarily delay and concentrate your resources to get rolling on the project while resisting unnecessary distractions.
4. *Principle of balance and momentum.* Use only as much time and resources as are needed to bring about the desired result. Unless hesitation is a tactic, never waste time taking follow-through actions.	*Awareness*: You may view productive actions as onerous, laborious, high-intensity maximum-performance efforts that are worthy of avoidance. Alternatively, what is the least effort you can make to produce the best outcome? *Action*: Challenge yourself to time and pace yourself as you follow through on the activity you selected.

TABLE 5.3 (continued)

Von Clausewitz Principles	Counter-Procrastination Applications
5. *Principle of boldness.* Go on the offensive and pursue each advance with vigor. Although there is no guarantee of success, advancing is positive. Unless they produce the best outcome, defense and retreat are negative.	*Awareness:* Decision-making procrastination is a practice of retreat, which is negative. The rational approach represents a policy of advancing, which is positive. *Action:* Consider how to use *challenge thinking* to advance your productive actions. Then practice thinking in the language of challenge as you proactively move to advance.
6. *Principle of efficiency.* Avoid trapping yourself between delays and deadlines so that retreat is no longer possible. It's better to avoid a problem than to extricate yourself from it.	*Awareness:* Delays resulting from indecision can put you in a pickle. If you let action lapse now, you can create a *later* problem that you may have trouble dealing with. *Action:* If the goal is to avoid extricating yourself from *being in a pickle*, plan to act starting now. Retreat is not an option.
7. *Principle of persistence.* Envelop the "enemy" and make the battle a decisive event. Allow no avenue of retreat. Disrupt enemy communications. Destroy enemy supplies.	*Awareness:* Each engagement with decision-making procrastination is a decisive event. Focus on the decisive action. *Action:* Go after decision-making procrastination weak points, such as urges to diverge. Disrupt the APD procrastination thinking process by challenging *later thinking.* Vigorously introduce a do-it-now process to overpower an urge to diverge.

Table 5.3 describes seven principles that I abstracted from von Clausewitz's book. His main message is to keep focused on what is important and to time and pace your actions efficiently. The principles and an application example are given in the table.

Here is a general principle for your battle to contest decision-making procrastination. You enter areas of uncertainty with a plan. Through executing your plan, you gain clarity and direction. You can apply this general principle (strategy) as you address both decision making and the other procrastination styles.

Forming the habit of acting decisively is rarely an overnight undertaking. It ordinarily takes a deliberate effort to familiarize yourself with a direct route to reasonable goals and action to get yourself out of a holding pattern. This *familiarizing decision* can get you out of an indecisiveness holding pattern.

End Procrastination Now! Your Plan

When you are choosing between positive alternatives of roughly equal value, the experiences that follow are likely to be different. All things being equal, no one can tell if the way that was not chosen would have been better or worse or about the same.

What three ideas have you had for dealing with procrastination effectively? Write them down.

1.

2.

3.

What three top actions can you take to shift from procrastination toward productive actions? Write them down.

1.

2.

3.

What things did you do to execute your action plan? Write them down.

1.

2.

3.

What things did you learn from applying the ideas and action plan that you can use in other areas? Write them down.

1.

2.

3.

6

Powerful Behavioral Techniques to Curb Procrastination

A strip of wallpaper is slowly pulling away from your wall. You decide to paste it back to the wall. But first you'll have to buy paste, get out your papering tools, and then paste down the wallpaper. You scratch your head. This seems like too much work right now. You'll get to it later. Meanwhile, you dig night crawlers for fishing and then go fishing. When you return, the wallpaper is still on your mind. Pulling nut weed from your lawn seems more appealing. Weeks later, you continue to find ways to delay. Is pasting the wallpaper strip a big deal? Absolutely not. You could do it while you are half asleep. Yet you find that the longer you put it off, the harder it seems to get started and finish.

Behavioral diversions are a distinctive feature of procrastination. To avoid discomfort, you play solitaire. Instead of concentrating and taking notes in a lecture, you doodle. And these are not just trivial substitute activities; behavioral diversions are a big part of health procrastination, where you put off developing healthy lifestyle habits that will increase your health and happiness.

These diversions are not always simply detours from making healthy lifestyle changes. Sometimes the results of these diversions become the bigger problem. You feel depressed. Rather than addressing the depression, you substitute drinking for coping, and problem drinking turns into alcohol abuse, which circles back to worsen the depression. If you are unaware of this cycle, you may not be aware that the drinking is a diversion. But you now have another significant problem habit that tracks with procrastination. Eating excessively can be a behavioral diversion from addressing anxieties, or used to fill hollow hours. After a while, you stop taking medication for preventing a coronary. It is inconvenient, and you'd rather eat chocolate instead.

Diversionary practices were known even in ancient times. Aesop had many fables to tell, such as about a rabbit who napped while a turtle passed by to win a race and about a grasshopper who fiddled the summer away while hard-working ants prepared for the winter.

If you are not diverting from your most pressing and important activity, you are not procrastinating. In this chapter, I will show you how to end behavioral diversions and use the time you gain to produce and prosper. You'll see how to sidestep behavioral diversions, make better use of time management information, apply an arsenal of cognitive and behavioral productivity techniques, boost your self-regulation skills, and harness the power of grinding it out when the going gets tough. Let's begin.

Behavioral Diversions That Lead to Procrastination

Behavioral diversions are a classic sign of procrastination. When you behaviorally divert, you substitute avoidance for productive actions. Instead of studying for tomorrow's test, you go to a party. Instead of dealing with an unpleasant conflict, you shop. Instead of overcoming your fear of making presentations, you decide to do some leisurely reading.

You can daisy-chain one behavioral diversion onto another. Instead of dealing with a knotty personnel problem, you check the latest news on the stock market. Then you browse a bookstore. You nap. You call a friend, and so on.

Paradoxically, productivity tools can be used as behavioral diversions. Computers increase productivity, but you can use them as a distraction to avoid an unpleasant situation by e-mailing friends, surfing online, and other such activities. Cell phones, PDAs, and text messaging are great ways to stay in contact with people, but they're also great ways to avoid work.

If you choose to trump a behavioral diversion(s), this ordinarily starts with knowing your options. To avoid automatically drifting in a procrastination direction, use the contrast exercise to sharpen your choice between behavioral diversions and *ending procrastination now*!

Behavioral Diversions	Ways to End Procrastination Now!
1. Play games or surf the Internet.	1. Take the first planned steps and use 10 minutes of playing a game or surfing the Internet as a reward for each hour of uninterrupted work.
2. Go for a drive.	2. Refocus and stay on task.
3. Call a buddy to chat.	3. Call a buddy to talk about ways of getting back on track.

Now it's your turn to identify your personal behavioral diversions and alternative actions to end procrastination:

Behavioral Diversions	Ways to End Procrastination Now!
1.	1.
2.	2.
3.	3.

Take this exercise to the level of analysis. The Greek philosopher Epicurus once advised weighing the results of an action against its side effects. Behavioral diversions can lead to excuses to get off the hook, strengthening a procrastination habit and leading you to live uncomfortably with an incomplete task. A do-it-now alternative may have side effects of strain from pushing through inertia, but this adds weight to your belief in your self-efficacy.

Is Time Management Really an Effective Behavioral Technique?

Time management refers to the use of time-saving ideas and management tools to increase efficiency. The approach involves analyzing how time is being spent, setting priorities, and planning and scheduling to concentrate on what is most important to do in the present moment. Better time management presumably provides an opportunity to capture added time for production.

Is time management a behavioral solution for procrastination? The process may be useful in contributing to the solution for some forms of deadline procrastination. However, time management is typically most useful for those who need the program the least. It also seems to be used to as a technique to squeeze more work out of managers and staff, and that presents a different set of problems.

There is another side to the productivity story. Research over the past two decades suggests that higher levels of productivity are obtained more through human resources programs that emphasize self-empowerment, extensive training, and teams that actually work well together. Productivity gains from these improvements exceeded those created by just-in-time, Total Quality Management, and supply-chain partnerships. It's tempting to conclude that a sense of control over your work is a critical factor in containing procrastination and increasing productivity.

In manufacturing settings, productivity is increased by doing more with the available personnel or doing the same amount of work with fewer people. Productivity may be measured by what a person does in an hour, and organizations typically shoot to get more done per productive hour. When you measure productivity against time standards, then increasing productivity follows efficient and effective time use.

Different jobs have different productivity expectancies. When they are applied to medical environments, production-line methods can detract from the quality of care. However, managed-care insurance companies rely on cutting down on the amount of time spent in physician-patient contacts and shortening the amount of time that it takes to process paperwork. This routine discourages the majority of new medical school graduates from going into primary care, where managed care can seem oppressive. It also increases the risk of burnout when one may feel like he or she is acting like a machine. From the perspective of a managed-care insurance company, one physician can be replaced by another, so burnout is a minor consideration. From a social and professional perspective, this is a serious waste of a finite resource, making this form of time management a nearsighted practice.

If you are a teacher, doubling the pace of your presentations may increase student burnout. Learning is a cumulative process, and developing new knowledge and skills is complex and takes time. However, a teacher may gain by avoiding procrastination on correcting assignments and planning lectures. Efficiencies gained in processing paperwork open more time for leisure activities.

In your daily life, keeping an eye on time can save costs. You avoid missing deadlines where you could face a stiff fine. You repair the roof before you also have water-stained ceilings to contend with. You fix your leaky car radiator before you have to replace a seized engine.

Maintenance delays reflect procrastination more than time management. Avoiding a crisis makes sense. However, procrastination can have a stronger magnetic pull. Here the issue isn't so much saving time as keeping yourself out of hot water. This is where you fall behind because of procrastinating and need to make excuses and seek extensions.

A big problem with time management is that you may procrastinate on applying the methods. If you do use them at first, you may back off from the techniques later. Moreover, this mechanical approach to structuring time doesn't address either the automatic problem procrastination habits in simple procrastination or the co-occurring conditions in complex procrastination. Other issues around the concept of time management include the following:

- Time management normally needs to be sold on the basis of the benefits of using the process to produce more for the same pay. When people view this negatively, reactance and resentment can balance any gains.
- Setting priorities is relevant to deciding what is first in line to do. However, a one-size-fits-all time management approach ignores the psychology of individual differences and differences in work conditions.
- Time management appears to treat time as a commodity and people as machines working on a timeline. This approach can undermine the intrinsic values a person sees in work by substituting a time management system for empowerment and self-control.

Time management may be useful in helping some people gain more value from time, but it is a watered-down approach for

---

END PROCRASTINATION NOW! TIP

Whenever you have an impulsive urge to diverge, think about the long-term hassles that can result from putting things off, and then think about your satisfaction when you act now.

addressing procrastination. The behavioral component may be helpful for some, but not necessarily for those who persistently procrastinate, who can profit from a comprehensive three-pronged approach.

Would Buddha Make a To-Do List?

If you asked Buddha how to obtain freedom from procrastination, he might say that you cannot desire freedom from procrastination because the desire would become the wall. You are the problem. Your ego takes up space. Don't desire, be desireless. Given this view, would Buddha make a to-do list?

Different people have different goals, values, philosophies, and spiritual interests. So, if you want to follow the path of Siddhartha to a higher spiritual state, then the world of commerce and achievement is not your cup of tea. Thus, you probably won't gain from a to-do list. You already know what you want to accomplish, and awareness and experience are your guide.

If you value improving your work performances, you are likely to operate with a value of self-development and improvement. The products you produce become the by-products of this process. So, you will rarely get far in any campaign to overcome procrastination unless you take steps to go beyond the phase of an enlightened awareness about the procrastination currents in your life. You have to get in the boat and row if you want to contest the currents and get to a more productive place.

The following sections give you behavioral steps for getting past diversionary processes and getting to and accomplishing more of what it is in your enlightened interest to do. Each action presents choices to reduce procrastination and use this reduction to gain a greater benefit. Is choice important? Choice appears to be correlated with increases in production and reductions in procrastination.

Thought Stopping

Playing the role of a psychologist in a brief Mad TV sketch, comedian Bob Newhart had the same solution for every harmful habit: "*Stop it.*" Does this "stop-it" approach apply to procrastination? Newhart was making a joke. But this can be a serious solution if it is used as a thought-stopping exercise.

Thought stopping is an accepted behavior therapy practice that can sometimes have a quick and a favorable result. Internally shout *stop* when you recognize an automatic procrastination decision (APD). For example, you hear yourself say, "Later." Immediately you internally shout, "*Stop it.*" You have little to lose by testing a behavioral thought-stopping exercise. However, plan to engage in what you'd ordinarily put off following shouting down an APD.

To-Do List

A *to-do list* is a catalog of items that you want to remind yourself to do. Using this organizing format, you may list items in their order of importance. The list may be a series of reminders, such as pick up the dry cleaning, get a gallon of milk, and call for a dental appointment. Some lists are templates for items that you routinely repeat: you want to remind yourself to stick to what it is important to do each day.

To-do lists can be short: one to five items. Short lists are useful when it is important to keep focused on a few important items. Throwing everything you can think of to do onto the list may be unrealistic, and you might bite off more than you can chew.

You can find different to-do list designs online. Some of them may be worth duplicating. You also can create your own list online and refer to it when you turn on your computer.

Your to-do list can combine items to do and behavioral diversions to avoid. Here is a sample form for you to complete:

Activity to Do	Done	Behavioral Diversions to Avoid	Avoided

Check off to-do items when they are done. This gives you a reference for your accomplishments. Check off behavioral diversions that you avoided. You make a gain each time you extract a procrastination keystone from a productive process and prevent this form of interference.

Cross-Off Planning Sheet

The cross-off planning sheet is a to-do list with a different twist. On the cross-off planning list, you cite the goal and list the steps. Then you cross off the steps as you complete them. Crossing off completed items can feel rewarding. Here is an example followed by a form for you:

Goal: Distribute information on a change in federal regulation.

Sequence of Planned Steps	Check When Completed
1. Obtain copy of new regulations.	
2. Write report.	
3. Submit report for editing.	
4. List-serve program execution.	
5. Execute distribution.	

Goal:

Sequence of Planned Steps	Check When Completed

Backward Planning

In backward planning, you imagine that it is a year from today and you are looking back over a very productive period. I'll use physical exercise as an example to show how this planning sequence works.

From this imaginary future point in time, trace back how you accomplished a priority goal to engage in physical exercise three times a week for 45 minutes a session. In working backward, you can say:

5. I worked out for a year, and I am in great shape and feel energetic.
4. I continued with my schedule, and I refused to cut myself any slack.
3. Before that, I entered the gym for the first time and began the program.
2. Before that, I phoned the fitness center and set up an appointment.
1. Before that, I accepted a feeling of discomfort as part of the process of going from where I am to where I'd like to be, and I stubbornly refused to substitute diversion for purposeful accomplishments.

Since the backward plan ends with the first step, you know where to start.

Backward planning has value when you visualize a result, but you rarely think about the steps that lead to the accomplishment. If you can visualize an outcome, then is it possible for you to visualize the step that came before meeting a long-term goal? Devising a plan is an important step in the process of changing from a behavioral diversion habit pattern to a productive pattern. Without preparation, you are vulnerable to a *promissory note* style of procrastination. Your plan helps you over the threshold from wishing to doing. However, you get the actual payoff when you execute the plan and persist with what you started. Once you have made the conceptual effort to go an extra step, it is simpler and easier to take concrete behavioral steps in the direction of your goal.

Organize for Efficiency

Organization systems do not, by themselves, curb procrastination. Nevertheless, these mechanical techniques can be part of a solution for operating with higher levels of efficiency and less stress caused by lost materials and shifting from activity to activity without finishing any of them (*rotating door procrastination style*). If you don't have a workable organizing system and you view yourself as not well organized, consider creating an organizing system to establish control over your routine. Here are some tips for building organization and efficiency into your routine:

1. Schedule time for recurring events (paying bills, cleaning, automobile oil changes, and so on), and follow the schedule.
2. Set aside a location for putting important objects in their place (keys, reading materials, bills).
3. Eliminate time-hog activities that consume a great deal of time but that yield little return (toss mail and e-mail advertisements and other materials with little relevance).

4. Delegate: hire someone to clean and take care of activities that cost you more to do than to farm out.
5. When feasible, order items online and have them delivered.
6. Schedule time for matters that require concentration when you are least likely to be interrupted.
7. If you are inclined to "forget" certain items nested within your system, use a reminder system. An elastic band on your wrist can serve as a reminder.
8. Avoid overorganizing or overscheduling your activities.

Behavioral procrastination can follow the development of an organizing system: you gather the information and set the system in place, then don't use it. Sometimes you have to push yourself to the next level of efficiency to get past a behavioral procrastination barrier. However, if you continue to bog down with this form of stop-start approach, ask yourself what you think is the underlying cause. Ask what you can do to move forward.

Self-Talk to Follow Through with Your Goals

When you talk yourself through the paces, you give yourself verbal instructions about what you'll do first, what you'll do second, and so forth: Now I will spell out my goal in concrete and measurable terms. Now I will lay out a plan to achieve the goal. Now I will take the first step in the plan. Now I will take the second step in the plan, and so on. Now I will review what happened and decide on adjustments. These instructions are covert, such as silently talking to yourself.

Using covert self-instruction accomplishes several results. You act to stop behavioral diversions. You substitute a proactive learning process for a procrastination process. You start sooner and finish faster. You benefit from improved performance.

Self-instruction may apply to improving sports performances. Sports psychologists John Malouff and Coleen Murphy found that golfers can improve their scores by giving themselves a self-instruction of their choice, such as "body stiff before each putt." Self-instruction also helps impulsive kids improve their school performances.

The Bits and Pieces Approach

The most complex challenges have a simple beginning. A person with a Ph.D. degree in theoretical physics started with simple steps in that direction. In a nutshell, the idea is to break it down and keep it simple.

You can break any complex task into a first step and manageable parts. Pretend that you are a project manager, and you need to break down a task for others to perform. What are the first, second, third, and subsequent steps? What instructions would you give to execute the first step?

Now, switch gears. Give yourself instructions, such as, "First I'm going to do this: _____. Next, I'll _____." Take the first step, and follow it up with a second.

Simplify the steps. The first step can be as straightforward as dialing a number for a phone call, booting your computer, opening a book, or getting out a pen and paper.

The Five-Minute Plan

Consistently use the five-minute plan to introduce a change to disrupt a procrastination habit process. First, commit yourself to taking five minutes to get started. After those five minutes, decide whether to commit yourself for another five minutes. You continue deciding at five-minute intervals (or another interval that works for you) until you decide to stop. When you are ready to quit, take a few added minutes to prepare for your next work session.

The five-minute system can be a surprisingly effective way to start intermediate- and longer-term projects. However, what if you put off the first five minutes? Regroup. Ask yourself what makes the task seem worthy of avoiding now. What are you doing to stop yourself from starting? The answers can point to a more basic problem that needs to be solved.

Tad couldn't get himself started on preparing an argument for a court presentation. The legal issues were complex. He was to face off against a senior partner from a large and successful law firm. Tad felt intimidated.

We talked about his anxiety about having his arguments torn apart in court. And since he was not yet clear on his arguments, Tad had to admit that he had no way of knowing whether he would be outgunned until he understood the issues.

The five-minute approach helped save the day. Tad agreed to take the five-minute approach to read the materials from von Clausewitz on preparation and how preparation can shape decisions. Five minutes wasn't such a long time.

Once Tad got the picture from me and from von Clausewitz's work, he applied the five-minute principle to gather information, research the law, and ask for help from other counsel. On the day of the trial, the high-powered lawyer that he had feared walked out of the court with egg on his face. Tad's argument was compelling and grounded. The judge complimented him on his superior preparation. Tad is a great fan of the five-minute plan. He calls it his friendly ally.

The Three-File System

Create a three-file system (you can create an e-filing system as well). Label the first file "catch-up." Label the second "keep-up." Label the third "get-ahead."

The catch-up file includes previously procrastinated activities that remain timely and important to do. Throw away whatever will not come back to haunt you. The keep-up file contains current activities, such as those that you might have on your cross-off list. The get-ahead file includes activities that, if you were to get a jump on them, could advance your interests and make your life easier later.

Spend time every day with your catch-up file and whittle it down until it's empty. Emphasize the keep-up file to prevent its contents from flowing into the catch-up file. Make time every day for your get-ahead file. This is where you work toward achieving what you envision.

We all have short-term tasks that get put off, such as canceling a dental appointment. If you need to cancel an appointment, do it when you think of it. This gets your mind onto something that is more productive to do. It also eliminates nagging self-reminders and making excuses for the last-minute cancellation.

A slight positive change in throwing off daily details can make a significant long-term difference. You can prevent small matters from becoming a crisis because they have been delayed too long. If you can't do something when you think of it, write it in a pocket notebook or record it. Then refer to the recording when you are free to respond. Then, do it the first time that you can.

Pulling It All Together

So far, you've looked at what you can do to go it alone as you organize and regulate your actions. Nevertheless, when you are confronting a complex procrastination habit, you may need all the help you can get. Who are the people in your life that you can call upon if the going gets tough? When you enlist help on specific procrastination issues, you may find that you have little need to call on them because you know that you can. However, a weekly check-in is a good rule-of-thumb approach to keep your buddy connected to and interested in your counter-procrastination efforts.

Get your act together and get rolling! Make a plan for how you will gear up for the change, and start the change in motion. Pick a start date. Publicly announce your intentions. Make a deal with a buddy to monitor your change program periodically. Start at the appointed date and time. Expect and accept making adjustments to your plan. Chart your progress. Routinely remind yourself about the long-term benefits you will gain and the long-term hassles you will avoid. Press forward.

Cognitive-Behavioral Correction Exercise

Procrastination can have a snowball effect: one diversion can roll over into another. In an earlier chapter, you saw how the ABCDE approach can be used to address complex forms of procrastination successfully. However, another powerful method is through a more comprehensive and structured cognitive-behavioral exercise.

Let's look at Brad's procrastination challenge, which surfaced when he was due to write a comprehensive report. The approach he took was different from his loose and avoiding style when he procrastinated. Doing the structured appealed to him.

In this exercise, Brad mapped his procrastination process, the change steps he would take, when he would start, and what resulted. As the saying goes, a picture is worth a thousand words. The following describes the process and results when Brad successfully came to grips with procrastination by following this plan. But first, let's look at some background information to put this program into context.

Brad had grown into the position of human resources manager for a rapidly growing insurance and financial consulting service company. The company employee handbook had originally been prepared by legal counsel with boilerplate materials. It was outdated and no longer suitable.

The company president wanted a comprehensive manual with graphic artwork, the company logo, a history of the company and its mission, and a state-of-the-art statement of company policies and procedures that conformed to state and federal law. Brad was the manager of human resources. He was the logical person to update the manual. He also had direct access to the company's labor lawyer and was one of the organization's best writers.

Brad had a different take on this. Because of the company's

rapid growth, he was overworked. The task seemed daunting and complex. He found writing the manual laborious, put it off, fell behind, and got two extensions.

Brad was concerned that his procrastination would get him fired. He was baffled. He stated that he was ordinarily well organized, but not for this project. He reported that he had materials piled up around his office. He had materials on policies on sexual harassment, bullying, sick leave, drug testing, health care, education, 401(k) retirement plans, performance reviews, progressive discipline, grievance resolution, and so forth. Downloaded materials were scattered in different sections of his hard drive. Materials and discussion notes from different meetings with legal counsel were scattered among the various papers. In a tone of exasperation, he said, "I got myself in a mess with the paperwork and with my job."

Brad had a complex form of procrastination. He worried about not living up to the president's expectations. He had high expectations for himself. He badgered himself for messing up his concentration by worrying about what he wasn't doing. He saw the manual as a showpiece for his company and a measure of his worth. However, regardless of the causes for his procrastination, Brad had a new deadline to meet, and this might be his last chance.

We talked about the triggers for Brad's procrastination and fleshed out a number of issues, including his high expectations and behavioral diversions to avoid his failure anxieties. He sheepishly confessed to playing Hearts on the Internet, and that was his biggest diversion. If he was overworked, he acknowledged that this was part of the problem. He lost time by playing the game and saw himself in a perpetual catch-up effort.

Brad caught on quickly about managing his expectations and separating his sense of human value from his employee manual–writing performance. He felt relieved when he saw that his worth was arbitrarily defined by his performance on the manual. However, he still had the manual to write.

From among the various ways in which he could organize his campaign against procrastinating, Brad decided on a procrastination mapping and correction approach. This approach included

1. Defining the process that he followed when he procrastinated
2. Identifying change steps that he would take
3. Determining a start time for each step
4. Identifying the results from executing each of the steps

Brad took five hours to think things out and to work up the plan. He completed the first three columns, leaving the results column blank. Because he would have to fit the writing into his normal daily routine, he estimated that it would take him 15 days to complete the manual. He then printed 15 copies of his cognitive-behavioral correction plan. He'd complete the results section at the end of each day. This approach helped him stay focused and served as a reminder of what he had already accomplished.

Table 6.1 is the first of the 15 procrastination cognitive-behavioral correction sheets that Brad completed.

Brad stopped playing hearts during his work hours, and changed his procrastination thinking and hair-trigger reaction by

END PROCRASTINATION NOW! TIP
CONTROL

Concentrate on shifting from behavioral diversion to purposeful action.
Orient yourself toward long-term goals and rewards.
Nip diversionary processes in the bud.
Transfer efforts from diversion to priority.
Reflect to ensure that you are tracking productively.
Organize your efforts to pursue your objective.
Leverage your productive efforts to gain advantage.

TABLE 6.1

Procrastination Process	Change Steps	Start Time	Results
1. Gathered materials on the employee manual without organizing the material. (Locating and relocating materials led to duplication of effort.)	1. Organize materials for each area into individual computer or paper files.	1. Right now, and stay overtime until this organizing phase is done.	1. Organized printed materials into folders by separate categories.
2. Purchased books on instructional design to help promote a better educational experience for the reader, then put off reading them.	2. Shelve the instructional design book readings until after the manual is written, then use information from these texts to improve the presentation.	2. Immediately set books aside.	2. Set books aside.
3. Feeling of discomfort when anticipating starting writing.	3. Label discomfort as an ordinary phase in starting a project where there is uncertainty and the task is time-intensive and unpleasant. Recognize that delays in organizing fit with a *contingency mañana* form of diversion that leads to distraction from organizing the compiled information and sidetracks the writing phase. Force self to start whether feeling like it or not.	3. As soon as an urge to diverge is obvious, use a slogan: "Discomfort is a false signal for retreat." Immediately counter procrastination thinking, such as "I'll get to this after I do more research" Rather than absorbing myself in the research plot, put my fingers on the keyboard and write.	3. Improved from total avoidance to producing better than 75 percent of the time. I stuck with the tension of writing without escaping into daydreams, calling meetings, or playing Internet games.

TABLE 6.1 (continued)

Procrastination Process	Change Steps	Start Time	Results
4. Divert to lower-value work activities, such as setting up meetings and e-mailing inspirational speakers about topics and rates.	4. Make list of common diversionary activities, recognize their purposes, and remind self of commitment to stick with the project; take reasonable 10-minute breaks every few hours to do diversion.	4. Start as soon as recognized. Use the urge to diverge as a trigger to refocus on employee manual. Follow work time interval with a behavioral diversion. (Diversions had to have some prior appeal; otherwise, why do them?)	4. Done.
5. Divert to Hearts game on Internet.	5. Burn a $100 bill for each five minutes of card playing during work hours.	5. Within 24 hours, collect 10 $100 bills and book of matches.	5. Stayed away from Hearts. Obtained the money, but it wasn't necessary to burn bills.
6. Tell myself I will get to it later, when I am ready.	6. Refuse to buy the rot that I'll be ready later. Raise questions about why later is better. Ask myself what it takes to get ready later that I can't do now.	6. Monitor thinking and execute strategy as soon as possible following awareness of later thinking.	6. Caught myself telling myself that later is better and asked myself to explain why this was so. Found no credible answer.

TABLE 6.1 (continued)

Procrastination Process	Change Steps	Start Time	Results
7. Tell self can't stand tension.	7. Think about thinking associated with the belief that discomfort is intolerable and address that issue by accepting and living with the discomfort.	7. Monitor thinking and execute questioning technique as soon as possible following awareness of can't stand tension thinking.	7. Had no rational answer. Still felt tempted to procrastinate. Forced self to start. Found it easier to continue.
8. Anticipate poor performance and experience anxiety.	8. What viable alternative results might be anticipated? Answer the question and keep with the schedule.	8. Monitor feelings of anxiety and respond at the earliest opportunity.	8. Feel more in control. Have less to worry about.
9. Daydream about great performance.	9. Concentrate on what I'm doing rather than on fantastic things that happen only in my head.	9. Stick with the schedule.	9. Less daydreaming. More accomplishments.
10. Figure out excuses to get extensions on the assignment.	10. Refuse to make excuses. Ask for extensions only under unavoidable conditions.	10. Deal with excuse-making situations as they come up.	10. Nothing to report.

introducing several measurable changes into his automatic process. As a by-product of changing the process, he changed the results.

Table 6.2 is a procrastination cognitive-behavioral correction sheet for you.

Self-Regulated Learning for Behavioral Follow-Through

Learning takes place in organizations, but formal educational opportunities may be thinning. These reductions don't diminish the importance of keeping up with your craft, profession, or job. Indeed, it is more important today than ever before to take charge of your own learning. However, when procrastination interferes with learning, it is wise to figure out how this happens and take corrective action.

Learning is a complex area. It's how you manage yourself in different learning conditions and when you are facing complexities that shape the outcome. Let's look at a self-regulated learning approach to advance your work when learning is a priority.

Self-regulated learning is an organized approach to learning. You have a learning mission and concrete goals. You think about your thinking (the metacognitive approach). You figure out how to achieve the goal, execute the steps in your plan, evaluate the results, and revise to add to your pool of knowledge. The research on this learning process supports its effectiveness. A self-regulated learning approach is associated with performing at higher levels and efficiently managing multiple complex goals requiring learning and the transfer of new information to achieve these goals. Corrective feedback strengthens this organic learning process.

By putting yourself on a self-regulated path, you take responsibility for how you learn. You pick the goals, the content, the time, and the effort you'll make. You decide the medium for learning, such as distance learning, a manual, a seminar, exploring and

TABLE 6.2

Procrastination Process	Change Steps	Start Time	Results

experimenting, observing others, and so forth. Self-regulated learning is a proven path to higher levels of accomplishment.

Early Learning and Aversion

Harvard psychologist B. F. Skinner saw diversions—inattention, daydreaming, and escape in the form of truancy—as responses to learning as aversive. He saw student escape and avoidance behaviors as emotionally charged with fear, anxiety, and anger.

You go through a long socialization process of learning to fit into your culture. This socialization process is necessary for an orderly society. However, it can have casualties, especially in the form of blame aversion procrastination.

You're an infant. You repeatedly hear sharp, emotionally toned corrective words like *no*. That *desist term* is directed toward correcting your behavior. If you heard the word *bad*, this is a *judgment term* that is directed at your character. Can early experiences that involve the internalization of negative words influence your perceptions and your willingness to learn? It depends on you, your perceptions, and the situations you may associate with learning adversities.

- Some judgment phrases may come across as forms of blame: "don't do that," "you should know better," "were you raised in a barn?" "how could you be so stupid?" "don't you ever listen?" A consistent barrage of judgment phrases can affect the way you act in certain learning situations. Behavioral diversion may be a solution for avoiding situations that you associate with defaming.
- A coercive "you should do this" or "you should do that" can grow out of early learning experiences. This coercive instruction may lead to compliant actions. However, depending on the situation and your perceptions, internalizing this coercion can lead to progressive malfunctioning in which you behaviorally divert from producing knowledge products.

- Judgment words and terms, such as "wrong" and "you shouldn't," can lead, in some instances, to wariness and timidness when it comes to learning.
- You may be the target of rhetorical questions, such as "why aren't you getting this?" This type of rhetorical question is normally intended to belittle and control. You may be leery of learning in situations in which you are evaluated by a person who is bent on intimidating and controlling you.
- Aversions can come in the form of omissions. Let's suppose that as a student, you observed other students getting praise and benefits. You're not in this loop. You may have felt and acted as if you believed the answer to the rhetorical question "what's wrong with me?" That negative view can influence your motivation for learning.

When negative learning experiences, memories, and beliefs prompt learning procrastination, you have the option of breaking an aversive learning cycle or continuing on a path where learning is aversive.

Breaking an Aversive Learning Cycle

Automatically holding back because of possible coercive criticism is self-limiting. A brief action exercise using self-regulatory questions to grease the skids for following through is on the next page:

Question	Answer
1. When you hold yourself back from learning something that is within your reach to grasp, what do you tell yourself as a reason to put it off?	1.
2. What are the exceptions to the above belief in which you engaged a challenging learning situation?	2.
3. What did you tell yourself that was different?	3.
4. If you believe that you can grasp the concept if you put in enough time, then what stops you from putting in the time?	4.
5. How do you develop a self-efficacy belief about learning?	5.

Controlling the conditions for learning can lead to learning. If you view yourself as being in control, learning is likely to be less averse. Here are some behavioral suggestions that support self-regulated learning actions where you control key conditions. These same techniques, however, also apply to other forms of procrastination where it is useful to create a structure to get something that is a pressing priority done:

- *Positive associations.* Associate something pleasurable with learning. You may enjoy classical music. When you are involved in learning, have classical music playing in the background. If you like a candle-lit bath, have a learning tape playing in the background as you take your candle-lit bath.

- *Premack's (1965) principle.* Here's the idea. If you follow something that you normally prefer not to do with a preferred behavioral activity, you are reinforcing the less preferred behavior with the preferred behavior. For example, follow each $^1/_2$-hour learning segment with something that you'd normally like to do. You may like viewing a five-minute Internet video segment updating you on your favorite sports team. You may prefer to stretch and run in place for five minutes, throw a ball for your pet, catch up on the news, or call a friend—anything you normally do that can reward a pressing and important learning process that you'd normally put off.
- *Intrinsic rewards.* You can give yourself your own intrinsic reward by verbally commenting "well done" for your learning and performance improvements.
- *Contingency contracts.* You write out a contract with yourself in which you give yourself a desired reward, such as treating yourself to a great meal at your favorite restaurant, for completing short-term objectives that are part of a longer-term goal. You penalize yourself for procrastinating by, say, writing a letter of praise to a politician you dislike or denying yourself your weekly night out at your favorite restaurant. You can benefit by finishing what you start, and that can be rewarding. You can gain a reward by avoiding a penalty (negative reinforcement). You gain the reward that you set for each phase of completion. However, the problem with contingency contracts lies in the enforcement of the penalty if you procrastinate on executing the contract.

Procrastination Exposure Training

Exposure training is the gold standard for overcoming fear. Procrastination impulses may track in parallel with brain anxiety and fear networks. This has yet to be assessed. Nevertheless, there is a psychological parallel between procrastination and anxiety and fear. Procrastination, anxiety, and fear are characterized by escape and avoidance actions.

You can set procrastination exposure training into motion by:

1. Agreeing with yourself that you'll endure your initial discomfort-dodging urges without behaviorally diverting
2. Taking on a timely activity that you put off
3. Approaching the learning task with the idea that you are going to work through the tension to get to the desired result
4. Exposing yourself to the tension that you normally try to put off experiencing
5. Showing yourself that you don't need immediate relief from tension
6. Sticking with the feeling and showing yourself that you can tolerate tension
7. Using your higher mental resources to guide your actions

Procrastination exposure training is not a one-time event. Benefiting from this exercise requires many experiences in different contexts with different forms and degrees of procrastination. Eventually, you can train yourself to use task tension cues as triggers for engaging in purposeful activities and undergoing behavioral follow-through.

If you come to tolerate—not like—the tensions that you associate with performing, you have gotten past a major hurdle to a productive and high-quality life.

Grind It Out

Psychologist John Goudy saw doing some disagreeable things as part of learning. He thought it was important to learn the importance of developing the habit of doing what is reasonable, whether the activity is unpleasant or not.

If you want a bigger reward and less long-term hassle, then grind out the work to get that result. Grinding takes toiling. Although grinding it out does not guarantee happiness or accomplishment, the process can dramatically boost your chances for a purposeful life that is filled with meaning and worthy accomplishments.

Remember, you can override the urge to diverge by following a structured plan to build and maintain momentum in a productive direction. This approach is simple. The process is rarely that way. However, you are likely to have fewer short- and long-term complications if you replace behavioral diversions with self-regulated actions and the do-it-now way.

End Procrastination Now! Your Plan

What three ideas have you had that you can use to help yourself deal with procrastination behaviors effectively? Write them down.

1.

2.

3.

What is your action plan? What are the three top actions that you can take to promote purposeful and productive outcomes? Write them down.

1.

2.

3.

What implementation actions did you take? Write them down.

1.

2.

3.

What things did you learn from applying the ideas and the action plan, and how can you next use this information? Write them down.

1.

2.

3.

7

Applying Techniques to Address Procrastination in the Workplace

The purpose of work is to accomplish something. *Work procrastination* includes putting off all or part of what you do to earn a living, and so you accomplish less.

Who engages in *work procrastination*? A percentage of those people who view their work as unpleasant and unfulfilling are likely to find ways to get around it: daydreaming, getting involved in office intrigues, going over the same ground, busywork, or withdrawal. However, while on the job, practically everyone will occasionally put something or another off. This includes people who are ordinarily conscientious, and in situations where procrastination can draw unwanted attention: "What happened to Charlie on this one? He dropped the ball."

Organizations treat *time shrinkage* as a fact of life; some of them even build this factor into their pay scales. The basis for adjusting pay to take procrastination into account is simple: it's virtually impossible to eliminate daydreaming, personal calls, taking time to work up to getting started, slowing down, and so forth. If an organization can recapture some of the *time shrinkage* that it has discounted, that's a gain. However, some of the dollar costs from procrastination can be especially serious. Delayed callbacks may result in lost business. Procrastination in adopting evidence-based personnel selection methods virtually guarantees selection problems that will inevitably come back to haunt the organization.

Most chief executives that I've spoken to about procrastination scratch their heads and tell me what currently bothers them about procrastination: a vice president who lives on the phone but doesn't have much to say; overdue performance reviews; talented outside salespeople who operate significantly below their capability; hand-wringing about introducing promising new products; energy expended in cover-your-tail activities and finger-pointing. However, a few believe that procrastination doesn't exist in their organizations. "We don't have procrastinators here (a 30,000-person organization). If we find them, we fire them." Who can seriously believe that any organization is a procrastination-free zone? Not me.

Consistent forms of procrastination can have consistent consequences. Doug is excellent at estimating automobile collision damage. However, he procrastinates on getting paperwork and reports into file folders. Multiple times during the day, he pressures himself by looking for estimates among scattered piles and in odd places. Michelle excuses herself from sitting down with a subordinate and talking about his pattern of calling in sick or showing up late on Mondays. She tells herself that she needs more information. Jimmy is an excellent carpenter, and his prices are fair. However, he dislikes making estimates and negotiating prices, and so he loses opportunities by default.

Doug, Michelle, and Jimmy procrastinate in different work zones. However, because of regularities in their procrastination patterns, members of this group don't have to reinvent the wheel to deal with their special procrastination twist. You can find tested cognitive, emotive, and behavioral strategies for ditching procrastination, as found in this book. The technology is getting better.

Procrastination may not jump right out at you. The costs don't call attention to themselves. Some of your coworkers' greatest source of enjoyment at work is connecting with one another about the latest office gossip, rumors, and criticism of the mistakes that others make. This discussion goes on in different ways throughout the day and often via the phone after work hours. Meanwhile, you're the *George* in "Let George do it." Your work motivation slowly declines as you think it's unfair that the burden falls on you, but your pay is no different from that of the gossip group. You hold back on a great idea because you don't want to draw attention to yourself. This holdback procrastination is a career limiter.

In this chapter, we'll look at procrastination in work settings. I'll start with why workplace procrastination takes extra work steps to curb. Then we'll move to *blame avoidance procrastination*. This silent procrastination trigger appears to be extensive. As procrastination can be a symptom of job dissatisfaction, you'll see how to align your preferred job functions with a job. I'll finish with a five-point management process to address procrastination.

Expect to Take Extra Steps

It takes extra steps to address work procrastination, and this means additional work. However, this is not much different from taking extra steps to take corrective actions to rid you of a debilitating inhibition, a general sense of anxiety, or an eating habit that leads to your being overweight. Believing that procrastination can be whisked away by a "just-do-it" solution is likely to be as effective as quelling a lifetime of anxiety by telling yourself, "just be brave."

If you want to overcome procrastination, it is usually wise to front-load your counter-procrastination work. Wishes and false promises to turn back a procrastination current support repeating a procrastination pattern.

Many of the methods given here apply to curbing procrastination as you learn to be a more effective you. Although ridding yourself of procrastination takes work, that is as it is. If you get out of shape, getting back into shape is not something that happens overnight. That, too, is as it is. Let's continue.

Can Work Procrastination Be a Symptom of a Larger Problem?

If you tend to procrastinate persistently at work, is this a general pattern that you'd take with you anywhere you worked? If so, then you have an opportunity to work out your procrastination problem wherever you are working at the moment. On the other hand, if procrastination is a symptom of your being in the wrong job, it is a symptom worth heeding.

Sarah loved looking at the plaques and awards that she had won for excellence in sales. She had a habit of keeping on top of things and richly deserved her awards. She thought that her next logical step was a sales manager position. She applied for the position at her company when it opened, and she got the promotion. That dream soon turned into a nightmare.

The management job was different from what Sarah had thought it would be. It partially involved a skill set that she already possessed, and partially a skill set that was not her cup of tea.

Sarah found she was great at advising individual members of the sales force on how to improve their performance, and at personally serving several key accounts. However, she was slow at or avoided reviewing reports, setting goals, designing staff training programs, and overall coordination of the sales force to achieve performance and sales objectives. She was weak on planning when this involved multiple staff members. Also, organizational politics presented Sarah with many unexpected challenges. Her former sales manager had been a master at finessing such matters and had shielded Sarah and the other salespeople from corporate politics. She was unprepared for competitive issues between herself and the managers of manufacturing, marketing, and accounting, each of whom had a deserved reputation as a bully. She was challenged getting her sales force to focus on issues, such as providing information on sales projections for their territories and completing sales reports.

Sarah was ambitious. A management job represented a step up in status and a higher salary. However, her new role brought to the surface multiple areas of difficulties that required her to function differently from the way she was prepared to function. Procrastination surfaced in every way, and Sarah eventually couldn't get out of the hole she dug for herself. Her procrastination was a signal that she was in the wrong job. She went back to sales. She dealt exclusively with key accounts. She returned to her old form of operating like an efficiency superstar because she was back operating in an area where she could influence the outcome. Once again, she created an excellent track record.

Ed did an excellent job as a chief of staff for a state senator. His career profile suggested that this was a viable career direction. He also had the temperament, interests, and skills to function effectively as an elected public official.

The senator decided against running for reelection. As a reward for his good services, the senator cleared the way for Ed to get a job managing a homeless shelter.

Once he was on the job, Ed did quite well in managing his relationships with local politicians. He enjoyed the exchanges and camaraderie. However, that was not his primary job function. Key managerial aspects of his job proved to be trouble spots.

Ed disliked dealing with union matters. He soon created contention between himself and union officials with his personnel policies and practices. He often violated the collective bargaining agreement and had a growing list of arbitrations to attend.

His deteriorating relationship with the union resulted in the union members following his instructions to the letter. This led to a slowdown, and the buses did not run on schedule. In a thin-skinned and defensive way, Ed sloughed off consumer complaints about the declining quality of services and maintenance. Lacking knowledge of the operation, he relied on his subordinates to manage the day-today operation. Unfortunately, most of them had also gotten their jobs through political connections and suffered from limitations in management acumen. A series of unfavorable news articles were the kiss of death for his career as a manager of a municipal bus operation. At that point, his political friends figuratively threw him under the bus. However, this was the best thing that could have happened to Ed at the time. He reentered the world of politics.

What went wrong? Ed got in over his head in an area in which he lacked executive management skills. He ticked off a powerful union. Rather than study ways to fix problems, he defended the current practices. He didn't replace managers who demonstrated inadequate capacity to handle the day-to-day operations. He skirted ways to meet customer expectations about timely services by taking his eye off that matter. This job was not his cup of tea, and that partially explains his procrastination across the spectrum of his primary job responsibilities.

Remember that the first part of ending procrastination is to become self-aware. Think about your procrastination habits at work and what's really causing them. Is procrastination a symptom of a larger problem? Could it be caused by job dissatisfaction or by another issue?

END PROCRASTINATION NOW! TIP
WORKS Plan

When starting a project, do the toughest or critical part first for effectiveness.

Organize your resources and order your activities for efficiency.

Regulate your thoughts and actions to advance your work plan.

Keep clear of needless distractions, such as procrastination diversions.

Stay with your strengths as they apply to the process.

Take stock of where you are in your career, where you'd like to head, and what you need to do to improve your chances for achieving your career goals. Here are a few questions to start the process:

- Are you currently in the right job and at the right level for your experience and talent?
- What is your potential for assuming additional responsibilities, and at what level?
- Would you need to prepare yourself now for either lateral or hierarchical advancement?
- What barriers are likely to be in the way, such as procrastination?

Your SWLO Analysis to Discover Productive Capabilities and Procrastination Hot Spots

Believing that you have work resources that you can rely upon increases job satisfaction. The bottom line is: you'll work productively where you align your talents and interests with a job and where you stretch to advance where you do best.

A strengths, weaknesses, limitations, and opportunities analysis (SWLO) is a strategic planning tool that organizations apply to position themselves to put their resources to the best use. You can use this method to focus your efforts on reducing procrastination by boosting your productive capabilities.

By visibly organizing information about your work resources, you'll find more opportunities to execute them. Using SWLO as a system to frame information about what you have going for you and what you can profitably avoid, you can sharpen your judgment about (1) whether you are on the right career track, (2) skills that you could transfer to a new job, and (3) strengths and talents that productively support organizational goals.

To complete the analysis, start with the three most important conditions for each area. Long lists invite procrastination. An example of such an analysis is given in Table 7.1.

TABLE 7.1

General SWLO Examples	Your Personal SWLO Examples
Strengths: What advantages do you have? (Examples: education; unique experiences; innovative ability; acting persistently with consistency) What do you do as well as or better than anyone else? (Examples: solve mechanical problems quickly; organize and control for efficiency; see new business opportunities and capitalize on what you see; persuade; innovate)	**Strengths:**
Weaknesses: Where can you gain the most by improving? (Examples: writing skills; communications skills; delegation skills; following through) What areas might you best defer to others? (Examples: activities that require technical skills; politicking; managing conflict; sales; organizing)	**Weaknesses:**
Limitations: What are your obstacles? (Examples: time; gaps in experience; financial resources; unavailability of competent coaches; lack of administrative support; changing conditions that keep changing; low energy level)	**Limitations:**
Opportunities: What patterns and trends merit action? (Examples: people procrastinating where efficient actions on your part give you an advantage; new product with potential; exercise and diet to improve attention, concentration, and energy; building reasoning skills to short-circuit issues)	**Opportunities:**

The weaknesses you identified in the SWLO analysis are potential procrastination hot-spot areas. You may have to deal with these matters regardless of the kind of work that you undertake. However, when you perform more of your preferred and fewer of your less-preferred work functions, you'll procrastinate less. Additionally, you can use SWLO to

- Identify areas that you can use to determine the closeness of fit between your strengths and your work.
- Sharpen your view about where you are likely to perform best and why.
- Identify or reinforce the value of the functions you perform that militate against procrastination.
- Identify work responsibilities to boost productivity when procrastination is not part of the picture.

Working in areas where your strengths apply lowers your risk of procrastinating, which can negatively affect your overall performance. Doing what comes easily, what you enjoy, and what you will work hard at is a formula for experiencing passion in your work, for generating successes, and for procrastinating less.

The Five-Phase Self-Regulation Program

Each new instance of a hot procrastination process is likely to have both familiar and unique features. Addressing each new episode effectively typically takes tested strategies and innovative new ones. The five-phase process can be applied to advance this initiative.

Up to this point, you've seen how to apply psychological strategies to reduce procrastination and make performance gains by using the time you save when you don't procrastinate. Now we'll look at how to apply a management strategy that you can use to regulate your efforts to help solve procrastination problems and also prevent them.

In using the five-phase self-regulation approach, your key is to identify productive opportunities that are impeded by procrastination hot-spot thinking and diversionary actions. This is a framework for coordinating basic management methods to prevent procrastination and to produce higher-quality results. The steps are to (1) analyze a procrastination situation, (2) set a direction, (3) create an action plan, (4) execute the plan, and (5) evaluate the results.

Problem Analysis

Analysis means breaking something down into its parts. This is a logical place to begin a procrastination prevention process. Information from the analysis flows to future steps, which involve organizing and coordinating your actions to break through procrastination barriers. However, the approach serves a dual purpose. You can also use it as a stand-alone productivity program.

Your answers to where, when, why, what, and how questions give you a way to look at the procrastination process from an analytic angle. Let's start here.

- *Where* are you likely to procrastinate? Do you put off maintenance activities? Do you back away from conflict? Do you fall behind on the latest information about your job? Do you delay preparing written work?

- *When* are you more likely to procrastinate? When you feel pressured? After lunch? When you are facing a complex challenge?

- Used in an inquiry, *why* invites analysis. Why do you procrastinate when you are facing some complex situations but not others? Why are you likely to follow through when a deadline is near? Why do you make false tomorrow promises to yourself? Why do you use excuses when you procrastinate?

- *What* types of conditions trigger your procrastination? What diversionary activities do you engage in? What follows the diversions? What happens next? What is the average length of time that you delay? What have you learned from this inquiry?

- *How* questions are directed toward accomplishing results. This is where you turn knowledge into know-how by stopping procrastination from interfering with the creation of high-priority work products. How do you address procrastination thinking? How do you emotionally tough it out? How do you behave differently?

Adding "and Then" to the Analysis. You can expand your analysis of procrastination by tracking procrastination with follow-up *and then* questions. The following describes the process.

Target: Putting off learning a new word processing program required for your job.
Reason: You believe that learning the program will be frustrating and you'll feel clumsy doing it.

Here's how the *and then* process can be applied to the sample frustration and clumsiness beliefs example:

- *And then?* I feel uncomfortable and insecure.
- *And then?* I want to do something else.
- *And then?* I promise myself that I'll get to learning the new program as soon as I can,
- *And then?* I busy myself elsewhere.
- *And then?* I nag myself about learning the program and feel stressed.
- *And then?* I keep finding other things to do.
- *And then?* I cram at the last minute.
- *And then?* My mind feels stuffed, and I have trouble focusing.
- *And then?* I swear I'll start earlier next time to avoid last-minute pressure.

The *and then* question-and-answer sequence can help you flesh out *what* you do when you procrastinate. It can give you concrete information that you can flow into a general counter-procrastination strategy.

Set a Direction

The five-phase self-regulation approach builds upon self-awareness and a problem-solving awareness and follows a sequence of steps that has often proved successful for profitable business enterprises. The process of setting a direction, however, starts with defining a mission and specifying your supporting goals that support the mission.

A *mission* to address procrastination is a special charge that you assign to yourself. It's a vision that gives you a broad direction. Some missions are so broad that they are perhaps too nonspecific and all-encompassing:

- Paving over the gossamer path of procrastination with self-mastery achieved by following through and performing at higher levels

- Shriveling the effects of procrastination by emphasizing productive actions to achieve performance goals
- Taking charge of my life by persistently following up on what is important to do

Positive missions to defeat procrastination are more precise. They say what you are going to do to achieve the things that are important to get done. Thus, they involve a two-phase process: (1) doing something (2) to achieve something. Here are sample missions that address specific procrastination conditions more concretely:

- Taking a public speaking class in order to improve expressive skills
- Increasing wellness through following a healthy diet and a moderate exercise program
- Contributing to the community by improving the welfare of handicapped children

A good general approach is to have a concrete mission. However, I've worked with people who preferred the general variety that are not popular with me, and did quite well. As the saying goes, different strokes for different folks.

What is your counter-procrastination mission? Write it in this box:

```

```

Set Concrete Goals. What is the difference between a goal and a mission? Losing 30 pounds is a goal, but a lifetime of eating balanced meals to promote health is a mission. Passing a test is a goal; learning to develop knowledge and wisdom is a mission. Getting a task done is a goal; operating with efficiency and effectiveness to promote productive outcomes is a mission.

In 1859, U.S. Senator Carl Schurz described idealized goals when he said, "Ideals are like stars; you will not succeed in touching them with your hands. But like the seafaring man on the desert of waters, you choose them as your guides, and following them, you will reach your destiny."

Our goals represent what we want to achieve. Setting and executing goals is one of the most reliably advantageous approaches to directing your efforts profitably. Concrete goals are generally more productive than the ethereal variety, such as to feel happy. Goals that are meaningful, measurable, and attainable are typically more useful than the abstract variety, such as saving the world from hunger. Here are four goal-development guidelines:

- Make your goals fit your mission. When your goals involve experiencing what you desire, you'll have a stronger passion for achieving them.
- Set realistic goals, ones that you can meet or where you can develop the ability to achieve the result that you seek. (Attainable goals are more likely to raise your motivation level than goals that you believe are permanently out of your reach.)
- Mastery goals are proficiency goals where you want to develop competence in an area of your interest. You can improve your personal competencies through mastering new challenges.
- Simultaneously use performance goals. These are results that you seek that are more limited and measurable, such as designing an efficient new manufacturing method to cap perfume bottles. The achievement benchmarks are the measured results of your efforts. Making 10 extra sales calls each week is an example of a performance goal. Performance goals typically lead to higher levels of performance.

Setting both mastery and performance goals is associated with a reduction in procrastination.

Within any dynamic organization, you'll have multiple and often competing goals. Time managers say that you should do the most pressing and important things first. This advice is rational but not necessarily realistic. The hyperbolic factor is likely to be present. The more pressing and important goal may be the one that was originally put off until the delays could no longer be tolerated. At that point, you allocate resources to the pressing task.

In a static world, you can better predict what is going to happen next. You know what to do first, second, and third. You'll allocate time and resources in that order. But we don't live in a predictable world where linear actions lead to goals.

In a dynamic world, which is more the norm, you'll sometimes have to reverse the ordering of your goals if you are directed to do so by higher authority. However, if your mission is to decrease procrastination in order to increase production, it doesn't matter that much if your priorities are shifted because of an external directive. The value of pursuing the mission and supporting it with achievable goals remains. You simply apply your counter-procrastination efforts to a different challenge.

Create Clear Objectives. When you break your goals down into concrete and measurable objectives, you improve your chances of achieving your mission. That is because smaller steps have shorter deadlines and the rewards of completion are closer in time. Thus they are more likely to get done. Objectives provide a sequence of activities. Finishing one step sets the stage for finishing the next.

Suppose you have procrastinated on working to overcome a fear of speaking before community groups. Your goal is to overcome this fear. You can break the goal down to five sample objectives:

1. Recognize powerless anxiety thinking, such as "I can't cope," and then look for exceptions to challenge this self-imposed verbal rumination.
2. Complete a public speaking course at a local college.
3. Research a project suitable for presenting before a community group.
4. Practice the presentation before a video camera to pick up and change any mannerisms that might distract from the presentation.
5. Present before a community group.

You can measure and achieve each of these objectives. For example, if you participate in a public speaking course, you have achieved that objective. Now, what can you do if procrastination gets in the way?

One Goal at a Time. You'll normally get better traction against procrastination if you pick one area where you procrastinate that is personally important to you and focus your efforts in that area. I've taken this approach effectively with people whom I've worked with who had hard-core procrastination habits. I used the same *one task one step at a time* approach with my graduate group counseling students.

Like the hard-core procrastination group, the counseling students took on an important self-development project they put off doing where each could make progress or complete before the end of the semester. Each had a buddy to report to and weekly progress reports that they submitted to me.

The following target areas show the diversity of challenges described by the hard-core and group counseling folks: completing performance reviews, finding a great new job, overcoming a fear of public speaking, getting better organized, completing assignments before a deadline, kicking a drinking habit, physical exercise, weight loss, saving rather than shopping, completing a dissertation, getting out of an abusive relationship, procrastination on stopping procrastination, and so the list goes on. Over a nine-year period, better than 90 percent achieved their objectives, as measured by confirmable results. Was this easy for each to do? Hardly. The students came away from the exercise with a deeper, personal understanding of what it takes to make an important personal change. I hoped that this personal experience would contribute to a feeling of empathy for the clients they would help who struggle with issues of personal change and development.

Why focus on one self-development challenge at a time? It takes time and effort to start and continue with any lifestyle change. Change is a process. As a species, we tend to be change-resistant when it comes to modifying what we are used to doing or find threatening. Developing skills in applying psychology principles to a self-management challenge and in applying self-management to help arrest a psychological challenge ordinarily takes time, resources, and effort.

Action Planning

It is the night of December 31. The hour and minute hands turn and meet for a fleeting moment at the number 12. With the sound of the chime, the New Year begins.

You tell yourself that this year will be different. You'll to to the gym. You'll turn over a new leaf on the job and get that coveted salesperson of the year award. You have a list of home maintenance tasks that are long overdue. They are now on your New Year's list of things to do. So, you give yourself a promissory note. Like so many others with you and before you, the note goes overdue.

Now 365 days have passed. The old year merges into the new. Not much has changed. Your sales performance was okay. You followed the same routines you did the year before. Your wish for a trophy whisked whimsically into the annals of irresolute resolutions as you clapped when the trophy went to someone else. You signed up and paid for the gym and then stayed away.

Draft a Specific Plan. What do the three New Year's resolutions have in common? They are personally selected and discretionary. Carrying them out would have some value; otherwise why decide on specific self-development goals? They involve goals, and perhaps a vague plan. However, people who make resolutions without deciding how they'll go about achieving the resolution (goal) risk procrastination.

You can love the idea of accomplishing your self-development goals. Sure, it would be great to manage conflict effectively. You'd be happy to shed an inhibiting fear. Losing weight looks like a good choice. Life could be easier if you were better organized. However, because you are responsible to yourself for the choice and its execution, you can usually find a way to give yourself an extension. You can also give yourself an excuse. Are you not the only person that gets hurt by such delays? That often-used rationalization to justify procrastination holds as much water as a lead ball.

If your promissory notes to yourself stay on the drawing board, this may happen for roughly these reasons:

- Weak commitment
- Underestimation of the ways in which old patterns interfere with the new ones you want to establish
- Lack of planning or inadequate planning
- Not building in counter-procrastination strategies
- Not planning for addressing procrastination about procrastination

When you procrastinate, you may have an idea for a productive plan that you can fall back upon. But that plan may be too general. If you want to tackle an entrenched form of procrastination, you'll normally do better if you formulate an organized plan that takes the cognitive, behavioral, and emotive aspects of procrastination into account.

Stay Flexible. I've seen many people stick to a plan when the circumstances had changed so radically that they figuratively were joining lemmings in a rush over a cliff.

Preparation is important, and so is being nimble and adaptive in the face of surprises. The *principle of acceptance of uncertainty* is that when the unexpected is discovered and needs to be managed, solutions may be invented "on the fly."

Unless there is good reason to the contrary, it is normally better to trust to your inventiveness when you are facing uncertain conditions, especially when unexpected events abound. The alternative is to play possum or join the ostrich with its head in the sand. However, putting your head in the sand won't stop what is coming your way.

The predictabilities in the procrastination pattern increase your chances of exercising control over the process, provided that you also establish control over the productive process. So, plan to address procrastination by introducing a competitive productive process.

Scenarios to Get Past Procrastination. Needless anxieties can arise from worrying about "what if situations," such as, "What if I were to fail?" What if I were rejected?" Because this form of scenario thinking reflects a sense of vulnerability and uncontrollability, it fertilizes procrastination, However, scenarios can prove to be highly productive, providing you pose alternative scenarios to yourself, extend the outcomes, and select the one that holds the best promise. In this form of productive scenario you focus on productive problem solving, the kind that can support constructive and sustainable change. Solving the problems through scenarios creates the framework for a plan.

You're thinking of creating a Web site to sell replacement automobile products for vintage Cadillacs, such as fan belts, spark plugs, and ignition wires. You plan to learn how to create and maintain the Web site, negotiate agreements with product manufacturers, determine what items to stock and what you can have drop-shipped, find out how to process credit card orders over the Internet, learn whatever you don't know about what you don't know, and so forth.

In one scenario, you gather the information you need, including doing a preliminary market analysis, and you look into how to finance the operation. The information you gather points to a low financial risk for a moderately profitable operation. You then bring a procrastination element into the scenario. You have a strong tendency to behaviorally procrastinate. You extend the scenario by analyzing the procrastination process and by creating a solution.

To behaviorally procrastinate, you have to have done something in preparation first. You find research and planning appealing. You determine that the project is viable. You find that fact interesting. However, you feel uneasy about how you'd handle Internet and phone inquiries about the products you sell. You don't like dealing with customer complaints and sorting out whether the returns were the result of preexisting damage or were customer-related.

Your history of bringing yourself to the brink of getting projects up and running and then putting off the execution phase is familiar. You recognize the emotional feeling of resistance to going further as you imagine executing the plan. From past experience, you recognize that your behavioral procrastination is a hard challenge to get beyond.

If you are going to behaviorally procrastinate, then except for the joys of doing the preliminary research and planning, it's less costly in time and resources for you to drop the idea at the start. The effort that goes into the research and planning phase in such a *set-up and stop* scenario might be better applied to a productive effort that you know you'll finish.

In a second scenario, you walk yourself through the preliminary phases just as before. However, you create a strategy for addressing the behavioral procrastination phase that you anticipate.

To get over this hump, you plan to make a public announcement of the launching of this new enterprise. You plan to throw a party to celebrate this new venture. You invite a group of friends, relatives, and acquaintances. You also know your history on the value of making a public announcement. When you make a public commitment, you follow through. You want to get past behavioral procrastination and deal with your execution uncertainties. If the numbers support starting the business, in scenario two, you'll take it to the public commitment stage.

Scenario three takes scenarios one and two into account, but also includes hiring someone to handle orders and customer service. Assuming that the execution of the complete plan leads to favorable results, this may be the thing to do if the plan proves economically viable.

Broadening Your Plan for Change. Having goals without plans is like traveling aimlessly without the benefit of a map. Planning is the step that prepares for the actions that you will take to achieve the mission that you seek by meeting the goals you establish. Planning that includes setting early start times is associated with a reduction in procrastination and an increase in productivity.

A plan is a blueprint for the steps you intend to take to move through the gap between where you are and where you want to be. However, the idea of planning can have about as much appeal as a diet of porridge. But is it really appealing to start with a promissory note for later actions and then excitingly run breathlessly at the eleventh hour to beat the clock? Few people I've worked with look forward to feeling pressured and frenzied at the eleventh hour.

Plans concern answers to at least these four questions: Where am I today? Where am I going? What do I need to do to get there? What alternative routes are available? They range from figuring out how you'll negotiate for an automobile purchase to something as complex as the Program Evaluation and Review Technique

(PERT). This is the planning structure that the U.S. Navy developed and used to produce the Polaris submarine.

You may not require a framework as elaborate as PERT to carry through with a physical exercise plan, to prepare to win a sales award, or to complete separate home maintenance projects. However, you can apply key steps to achieve your target goals. Here is the gist of the PERT plan:

1. Identify specific tasks and milestones (start dates and completion dates for each phase).
2. Determine the ordering of the activities, including which tasks can be done in parallel and which depend on the completion of other tasks first.
3. Estimate the amount of time required for each activity (expected time, most optimistic outcome, and most pessimistic outcome for meeting deadlines).
4. Determine the total time required (add up the times for each segment to estimate the total time).
5. Update PERT as the project progresses (modifying the process as actual times replace estimated times and adjustments are made on resources and their allocation).

PERT plans are useful for addressing timing and pacing issues. The model applies to maintaining a productive momentum to avoid last-minute time crunches, simplifying the activities in complex long-term projects, and positioning yourself to control the process by controlling the schedule.

Organize for Action. As any useful framework for planning might do, PERT provides psychological coat hangers on which to hang information about goals, objectives, and resources. You supply the judgment on when and how to apply them through actions such as setting schedules, identifying outside groups to support the process, and determining when those groups will be brought into play. This preliminary work takes both time and resources. However, when you are facing a well-practiced procrastination habit, the time you take to work out the details can save you considerable effort and time and reduce needless hassles that can come later. You won't know what is missing from the plan until you take the steps along the way. If you wait for perfection, it will probably never come.

Now it's your turn to devise a plan. Here is a modified sample PERT planning framework for building counter-procrastination measures into a productive process.

Goal: _____.

Your Counter-Procrastination Plan

Activity Sequence and Time Estimates (what to do first, second, etc.)	Start Date (for each phase)	Completion Date (for each phase)	Reward for Completing Activity	Strategy for Containing Procrastination

Can you avoid procrastination by emphasizing meeting performance objectives as outlined in the first column of the plan? Will setting start dates make a positive difference? Can setting interim deadlines for each activity make a positive difference? Will mindfulness of procrastination and planning for procrastination make a positive difference? These questions can be answered through what you do to execute the plan.

Execution

Execution is easily seen. It is what you do to follow your plan outline. This is the time in the five-phase process where you test your plan to see what works, what doesn't, and what has potential if it is modified to fit the situation. A payoff is that you achieve the goal you set out to accomplish.

Execution implies motivation. However, where does the motivation come from? Is it from a lifetime of conditioning in which you learned to set and execute goals and then stretch to reach for them? How does this achievement motivation differ from chipping at a piece of flint to create a spearhead or gathering grain to store for the winter? When does the motivation start?

A common procrastination trap is waiting to feel inspired before you start. This puts the start time out into an indefinite future where the proximity of a deadline can trigger frenzied activity. You are likely to experience motivation if you set a short start date and then take the most basic steps. Even if you plod through the process without feeling that motivated, you'll have accomplished what you set out to do.

When you accept the dual challenge of following though on what you believe is important to do and facing an old procrastination foe, you can expect to experience reluctance and to resist getting on the do-it-now path. However, when you voluntarily subject yourself to the initial discomfort, you do so to help you achieve a longer-term goal of plowing forward against a sea of resistance until the resistance fades. Expecting and accepting discomfort as a part of the start-up phase is a start in the direction of greater self-efficacy. This step also helps train the mammalian brain (the horse) that discomfort is not dangerous.

What can you draw upon to bridge the gap between waiting and acting? When you start a productive process and a resistance arises, look to your resources from your SWLO and career congruence lists. What do you have going for you that can be matched against the emotional resistance? Is it flexibility, innovativeness, and resourcefulness? Can you call upon conscientiousness, common sense, and knowing how to profit from wise advice when you ask for it? By intentionally shifting from procrastination thinking and emotional resistance to applying what you have going for you, you can tip the balance in favor of accomplishment over procrastination.

There is rarely a quick and easy way out of a procrastination habit. Making meaningful personal changes is often like slogging through a knee-deep swamp. The wading is not easy. However, if you don't slog your way out, the chances are that you'll stay stuck. If it turns out that you move with a fleetness of foot that surprises you, so much the better.

Evaluate Your Progress

We can separate evaluation from execution, but only artificially. Thus, the entire five-phase program is an interactive and organic process.

At different phases and points in time in the process of execution, missions, goals, plans, and evaluation form a grand convection in which the critical elements come together. You stick with the system when experience shows that you can make it work effectively. Changes come into play when it is clear that you'd be wise to try another way. This happens when parts of the plan are not workable or it would be too costly to make them work.

Evaluation as Feedback and Guide. Evaluation is a form of feedback and guidance that gives you a measure of change and a basis for adjusting what you can next do to further your goals. Here are some feedback questions:

1. Have I accepted responsibility for taking the initiative and following through?
2. What have I accomplished by following a process of mission development, goal setting, planning, and executing strategy?
3. What have I learned that can further support my antiprocrastination campaign?
4. How can I apply this knowledge?

Consolidating Your Five-Phase Self-Regulation Program

The following table pulls together problem analysis, setting a direction (mission and goals), plans, execution, and evaluation. In the five-phase column, you spell out what you're doing in each area. Then you note what you learned by following the process.

Your Five-Phase Process

Five-Phase Management System	Learning from Actions Taken
Problem analysis	
Direction	
Action plan	
Execution	
Evaluation	

End Procrastination Now! Your Plan

Careers and jobs are rarely perfect. However, since you spend a significant part of your life at work, why not accomplish what you can capably do in a reasonable way? By regulating your actions to exclude procrastination, as a by-product you're likely to accomplish more and have fewer regrets. You'll have more favorable things to report when you write your autobiography. Use the key idea and action plan to record what you've learned that can flesh out that autobiography.

What three ideas have you had that you can use to help yourself deal with procrastination thinking effectively? Write them down.

1.

2.

3.

What is your action plan? What are the three top actions that you can take to contend with adversity and propel yourself into positive territory? Write them down.

1.

2.

3.

What things did you do to implement these actions? Write them down.

1.

2.

3.

What things did you learn from applying the ideas and the action plan, and how can you next use this information? Write them down.

1.

2.

3.

Appendix

Sample Therapy Script for a Procrastination Scenario

Ted was 40, married, and the father of two preteen daughters. He worked as a sales manager for a small manufacturing company. The company atmosphere was friendly and cooperative. His presenting problem was procrastinating on completing performance reviews.

For the third year, Ted was three months behind on completing his performance reviews. In the previous two years, his manager had completed them and gone over the results with each member of the sales force. This year was different. Ted could either finish the reviews or look for a new job. His manager gave him six additional weeks to finish, provided that he worked with an expert on overcoming procrastination. Both Ted and his boss simultaneously conferred with me over the phone about the seriousness of this matter.

Ted loved many aspects of his job, but not the performance reviews. His wife and daughters loved their home and their neighborhood. They preferred that he keep his current job. They had no interest in relocating. However, even though Ted had made many promises to himself and others to do the reviews, he hadn't started. When he thought about starting, it was as if he had come up against a wall. Ted was eager to get help with his performance review procrastination.

The following interaction was edited to eliminate background information and diagnostic checks, to change identifying information, and to improve readability. It is broken out into two sections: (1) the therapeutic interaction and (2) comments on the CBT therapeutic process. Thereafter, you'll find a summary of additional steps that Ted took, and the outcome.

Interaction	Process Comments
Bill: Ted, tell me about the performance reviews.	Obtain client's perception of the presenting problem.
Ted: Dextron (not the real name of the company) keeps me hopping. I'm too busy to get to the reviews. Besides, everyone knows that the reviews are a crock. They're just busywork. They're a waste of time. I can sell and my people can sell, and that's what's important. But I want to keep my job. I can't believe that I let it go this long.	
Bill: That doesn't surprise me. Procrastination is an automatic habit that can go on like it has a life of its own. This is one of the more challenging problem habits for people to deal with. Practically everyone has at least one area in which he feels burdened by the habit and feels baffled about why he can't just do something to start and finish. This may happen when a change takes place, and for some, adjustments can prove challenging. In your situation, the change was the introduction of the performance review system.	Provide educational information. Destigmatize procrastination. Treat the issue in a matter-of-fact way. Affirm the reality that procrastination can be a tough habit to break.
Ted: I'm relieved that you said that. I thought it was just me.	

Interaction	Process Comments
Bill: Let's see if we can figure out what is going on. Let's start with your view that performance reviews are a waste of time.	Set the stage for problem solving.
Ted: Yeah, they are a waste of time. I have better things to do. I shouldn't have to do them.	Problem clarification. Get the client's perspective on what's required. Log the client's "shouldn't have to do it" belief for later use when the timing is better for clarifying or dealing with this issue.
Bill: What do you do for each review?	
Ted: I have to fill out a rating scale and make general comments.	
Bill: On average, how long does it take to complete each review?	Gather information on time commitment.
Ted: It takes half an hour to do and half an hour to give the results.	
Bill: So would 20 hours be a realistic estimate for the reviews for all five salespeople and your assistant? That would include putting together the information and handling rescheduling issues.	
Ted: I should be able to get them done in less time than that.	
Bill: So the amount of time it takes isn't as much the problem as what you make of the reviews themselves. Are performance reviews part of every manager's assignment?	Clarifying Ted's idea for what he should be able to do is tempting to address. This is a timing issue. It's also a tracking issue. So I stuck with the theme to avoid sidetracking. I'll deal with Ted's meaning of "should" later.
Ted: Everyone has to do them.	

Interaction	Process Comments
Bill: I understand that performance reviews have been in place for a few years. What's your understanding about their use?	
Ted: I think we put them into place for several reasons. We had no objective performance standards. We wanted to keep track of how well our people were doing. Our corporate legal consultant recommended that we have a way to justify both disciplinary actions and bonuses and promotions. She said that our company had grown large enough that we needed a way to be sure that the appraisals were job-related and based on measurable and reasonable standards. It was important for employees to have a pathway to appeal their reviews if they disagreed with the findings. The reviews provide a basis for performance improvement plans. I guess they make some sense. But I still don't like doing them.	
Bill: It sounds like you have a clear understanding of their purpose. I agree, you don't have to like every part of a job.	
Ted: Okay. Now we are getting somewhere. You've agreed that I don't have to like them.	
Bill: Right. But your job is on the line for not doing them.	
Ted: I know. I have to get them done. But I shouldn't have to waste my time doing them.	

Interaction	Process Comments
Bill: *Should* is one of those words with different meanings. One is a reminder: I should remember to buy a loaf of bread. Another is a tyrannical or coercive *should*. If you think that the reviews are unfairly dumped on you, that they are a waste of time, and that you should not be required to do them, you might view them as taking time away from what you'd like to do and feel resentful and resist doing them. Another view is that you should live up to your standards by doing whatever you undertake perfectly well. So it isn't the word so much as its context and what it means. If you use *should* as a reminder, you'll probably feel differently from the way you would feel if *should* meant that you *must* do performance reviews. Of these three views on *shoulds*, do any fit?	Client repeats the idea that he shouldn't have to do them and that they are a waste of time. The timing seems better for probing this issue. Clarify the potential key word *should* to determine whether it represents an expectation or is used conditionally. The waste of time idea can be explored later.
Ted: (Long pause) It's funny that you put it that way. I think it's two ways. I resent doing them. But I think that if I must do them, I want to make them really meaningful for my people. I want them to make a difference. I want my people to have new insights into how to be super salespeople.	
Bill: And when you think you must make your performance reviews meaningful, what follows that thought?	Ask clarifying question that may establish a link between expectations and potential emotional consequences.
Ted: I think they'll be disappointed.	
Bill: Because?	The question invites Ted to expand the issue and for me to better understand his perspective.
Ted: (Pause) I won't do well enough. I'll get criticized.	

Interaction	Process Comments
Bill: And how do you feel when you think that way?	Check for a connection between thinking and emotions.
Ted: Tense, depressed, miserable.	
Bill: It sounds like you have high standards for yourself.	Inference from data.
Ted: I've always had high standards. My mom used to call me Mr. Perfect.	
Bill: When you think about the performance review and view yourself falling below standard, what do you think about yourself?	A check on a potential self-concept issue.
Ted: (Pause) Like a loser and a failure.	
Bill: Perfectionist thinking involves the idea that if you don't do well enough at what you think you should do, you're a flop. Others will think ill of you. When you think that way, do you feel anxious about the possibility of performing poorly?	Raises question about perfectionist thinking and its relationship to a performance anxiety.
Ted: That sounds about right.	
Bill: So, you're either a winner or a loser. Is there anything that may lie in between?	Expand on the binary thinking issue and show an alternative perspective.
Ted: (Laughs) A partial loser?	
Bill: It's better to laugh about what lies in between than to take the extremes seriously. But you can also consider that you are a person who is challenged to find a way to break through a procrastination barrier. Meeting the challenge becomes the issue. That gets you away from making character generalizations about yourself, and this may help you fix your focus onto solving the problem. By the way, is there any universal law, other than Ted's law, that requires you to be perfect?	Summarize. Continue to question perfectionism.
Ted: No. I hadn't thought about it that way. Can I appeal Ted's law and change it?	

Interaction	Process Comments
Bill: Hey, you're the judge who interprets that law. You can change it anytime. Do you think you put off doing the performance reviews to avoid failing?	Presenting the connection between perfectionist thinking, fear of failure, and putting off the reviews.
Ted: It's beginning to sound that way.	
Bill: Is having your reviews challenged part of this picture?	Raise the issue that people with perfectionist views may also suffer from anxiety over disapproval and confrontation anxiety.
Ted: I worry about that.	
Bill: What would it mean if you had your reviews challenged by one of your people?	Question to probe connection between a contingency between performance and self-worth.
Ted: They'd think I was a jerk. I'd lose respect.	
Bill: And what would you think about yourself?	Question to get back to the core self-concept issue: what Ted thinks about himself.
Ted: That I'm a loser.	
Bill: You'd have to be a mind reader to know what others think. But even if you were right, and some people thought you were a jerk, would that make you one? I mean, if someone called you a green grasshopper, would you start eating grass?	Attempt to defuse Ted's tendency to overgeneralize about his worth by suggesting an alternative perspective.
Ted: (Laughs) I've been called worse than a green grasshopper. I guess what you're saying is that I am exaggerating, but that even if I'm right about what people think, I'm still making too much of it.	

Interaction	Process Comments
Bill: Ted, I think you're right about exaggerating. You may influence but can't control what others think. You probably don't want to go out of your way to cause people to think badly of you. But you can't win them all. Now, what about other managers who sometimes have their reviews appealed? Are they losers?	Clarification for promoting an alternative perspective.
Ted: No. My friend John had two appeals this go-round. The two people complain a lot. He reported that they complain too much. They complained about that part of the appraisal, and their complaints helped validate John's point. John's not a loser. He's one of the most straightforward and fair people that I know.	Question identifies an exception to Ted's view that criticism = loser.
Bill: If John is challenged and still is fair, what would make you a loser if someone challenged your review?	Reframing the issue with an incongruity intervention: what does the disparity mean?
Ted: (Long pause) I hadn't thought about it that way before.	
Bill: How so?	Clarification question to test for understanding.
Ted: It's hard for me to accept being imperfect. Yet I accept that it is all right and normal for others not to be 100 percent right all the time. Maybe I need to rethink my position.	
Bill: How you go about rethinking your position can make a difference. If you work to accept yourself as a fallible person who is working to do better, then you may look at procrastination as an interference that you can work to stop. You'll have plenty of opportunities to practice. The performance reviews will go on. But if you don't want to do them and the performance reviews are part of your job description, what are your options?	Introduce change as a process; encouragement; determination of client's understanding of his choices.

Interaction	Process Comments
Ted: One is to find another job where I won't have to do reviews. Another is to ask for a demotion and let someone else do them. I could learn to stop procrastinating on doing my performance reviews. I'd rather keep my job. There is a lot about it that I like.	
Bill: You spit that out pretty quickly. It sounds as if you've given your options some thought.	
Ted: Absolutely. But there is only one good option for me: get them done and keep out of hot water in the future.	
Bill: Okay, then the goal is to keep your job, and this starts with finishing the reviews and avoiding this sort of problem in the future.	Strongly reinforce client's rational goal.
Ted: That's my best option.	
Bill: Besides *should thinking* and failure fears that can start procrastination in motion, procrastination can start with any perception that triggers discomfort of any sort. It also can be an independent problem habit that takes an extra effort to stop. Let's see what's going on when you procrastinate. When you think about your performance reviews coming due, what do you think?	Summarize and continue to educate about procrastination.
Ted: I feel like I don't want to do them.	
Bill: And then?	A question to cause Ted to think more deeply about the process he follows when he procrastinates.
Ted: I do something different.	
Bill: For example?	It's easier to work with examples than with speculative interpretations.

Interaction	Process Comments
Ted: You name it. I start filing old sales reports. I call my wife to talk about the kids. I do some joint sales calls. I check the stock market. I meet with other department heads. I sometimes close and lock my office door and nap. I fantasize about buying a business and having others do the performance reviews.	
Bill: It sounds as if you've got that part of procrastination pinned down.	
Ted: Yes. I skimmed your book on procrastination before this meeting. The section on diversions got my attention. I said to myself, My God, that is what I do. I think I know I'm procrastinating. It's almost like I'm doing these things without thinking about what I'm doing. It's hard to explain. I know I'm sidetracking when I do these things, but I don't seem to be able to stop myself.	Putting himself out of the way to gather information and prepare for his session suggests that Ted feels motivated to change. Or at least motivated to impress the therapist.
Bill: Is there anything that you are aware of before you sidetrack yourself?	Check on intervening variables, such as what Ted is thinking, that goes between his awareness of the performance review and his task-avoidance behaviors.
Ted: (Pause) My body tightens, and I feel really resistant about starting. Sometimes I feel really tired.	
Bill: Do you have any thoughts about the reviews?	
Ted: Yeah. Like I said, I start thinking that they're a crock and a waste of time. I know I'll have to do them. I'd just rather do them later.	There are many choice points in therapy. Rather than deal with reviews as a "crock," I checked on *later thinking*. However, following up his views of the reviews is also valid.

Interaction	Process Comments
Bill: And when later comes, what normally happens?	
Ted: I continue to put them off.	
Bill: Do you think of anything you can do to prepare for the reviews?	Question to see if *contingency mañana* thinking is present.
Ted: I need to read up more on how to do a better review. Then I'll get to it.	
Bill: That's known as the *contingency mañana* way of thinking. You'll get to it after you do something else first, like reading up on reviews. Do you read up on the reviews?	
Ted: (Laughs) Nope.	
Bill: And when you run out of time with the performance review, what happens?	
Ted: I ask for an extension. I say I was too busy helping salespeople and customers. I ran out of time.	
Bill: What happens then?	
Ted: I get into hot water. I'm six months behind on the reviews. No one believes me.	
Bill: Ted, what have you gotten out of what we've talked about so far?	It's useful to check the client's understanding periodically.
Ted: I feel uncomfortable about the reviews. Rather than starting them, I do something different. I end up with my back to the wall, making up excuses that my boss doesn't believe. I think that I have to stop telling myself that I'll get to the reviews later.	Ted shows that he has a good grasp of what he does when he procrastinates.
Bill: It will normally take more than an awareness of this process to get the performance reviews started and finished. But you have to start somewhere if you expect to finish the reviews. What can you do to start the ball rolling?	Focus Ted's attention on the behavioral assignment phase.

Interaction	Process Comments
Ted: I'll get to work an hour early and start writing. I won't go home at night unless one report is done.	
Bill: Is that a new idea?	Since Ted's plan doesn't sound like a new idea, I decided to check on past results.
Ted: No. I've told myself I'd do that before.	
Bill: How has that worked?	
Ted: It hasn't.	
Bill: You could try that approach again and apply what you've learned today. Simultaneously, you could work on your perfectionism, specifically your belief that a less than perfect performance review defines you as a loser. To keep perspective, you can match that belief against what you said about John. As an alternative to perfectionist thinking, look for evidence to support a view that you are a person who is in the process of development and that it will take time and practice to improve your ability to do reviews.	Suggest how an old approach can be done in a new way. Expand on the person-performance distinction.
Ted: I like the idea that we are in phases of development. That feels better.	
Bill: Changing the procrastination process can be challenging. To start, you could leave a message on my answering unit to say what you learned each day about dealing with performance reviews. You could say something about your progress, and what you did to deal with your discomfort avoidance urges, procrastination thinking, and diversions. If you hit a snag, we could discuss it on the phone.	An invitation to call to deal with the problem as it is occurring.
Ted: It's interesting that I'm worried about wasting time and then I waste time worrying. I get it about perfectionism and either-or thinking. I'll do at least one review a day and call you if I start to procrastinate.	Ted insightfully comes to his own conclusion about the "waste of time issue." Behavioral assignment is set by Ted.

Interaction	Process Comments
Bill: As you approach the performance reviews, think about what you do when you procrastinate. By tracking this process, you can make it less automatic and put yourself in a position to evaluate and change it. The issue is the performance reviews. When you think of the reviews, you feel uncomfortable or fatigued. You tell yourself that they're a waste of time. But that sounds like subterfuge. It sounds more like a fear of doing an imperfect job and getting criticized. Your perfectionism sounds like a main issue, where you make your worth depend on your performance and you set yourself up to fail by avoiding the task. It sounds to me like the performance reviews are a threat to you. The diversions distract you from what you fear. There is a practical issue of getting the performance reviews done to keep your job. The perfectionism issue seems to be in the way. What do you think?	This summary lays out a rational emotive ABC framework for organizing information.
Ted: I get it. I can see why you said that procrastination can be baffling. I've had my eyes glued to the trees and couldn't see the forest.	
Bill: It seems to me that you have an opportunity to do two things at the same time. You can work on your perfectionism as you work on the performance reviews. You could get a double benefit for yourself. You can help yourself get rid of two sources of stress, procrastination and perfectionism. While we were talking, I mapped out a way for you to attack perfectionism as you take on the performance reviews. (Hands Ted an ABCDE framework that is filled out with Ted's data.)	Identify the double benefit of dealing with coexisting conditions simultaneously. Using Ted's information for how to use the ABC form makes it directly relevant to him.
Ted: (Pauses and reads the material) Okay, I like the idea that I can make two gains.	
Bill: Our time is nearly up. Are there any questions you want to ask?	
Ted: Nope. I've got a lot to think about and performance reviews to do. Same time next week?	
Bill: See you then.	

Follow-up and General Comments

The therapy session fleshes out issues that you may find helpful when you are working with a client whose presenting problem is procrastination. The transcript uniquely shows how to separate and deal with both procrastination and coexisting conditions. But, as you may suspect, Ted still had a great deal of work remaining to get past his procrastination barrier.

Procrastination Complications

If Ted completed the performance reviews, what was next? For some people, completing a delayed task means that there is one less thing to do. In Ted's case, finishing the reviews had an additional implication.

Ted experienced an *evaluation anxiety*. He feared that his staff would have bad reactions to his reviews. Not wanting to make a mistake, and having a strong need to be liked, Ted felt uncomfortable discussing performance problems with the members of his staff. That contributed to his procrastination.

By avoiding the reviews, Ted avoided telling other people what he thought they might not like to hear. He also feared that he would not achieve his fantasy goal: to make the reviews so meaningful that he'd be exalted. So Ted's procrastination was partially connected to anxious anticipations.

The dreaded performance discussions were on a time dimension. Ted had time to prepare. But his preparation was to avoid rather than to cope. His preparation involved fantasies about perfection. Then he delayed seeking the level of perfection that he suspected he could not attain. And if perfection was a contingency for action, and perfection was impossible, then procrastination was a predictable outcome.

The law of parsimony says that the simplest explanation is preferable to a more complicated one. A simple explanation is that Ted felt discomfort when he anticipated doing the performance reviews, then ducked this discomfort by sidetracking himself into less pressing pursuits. However, you can practically always find complications that weave through a problem process. Bringing them up and dealing with them may be the most direct route out of a mental jungle filled with diversionary dead-end pathways.

Continuing the Process

Ted's perceptions of the performance reviews included a combination of a discomfort dodging, perfectionism, and procrastination in which each amplified the others. Ted's goal was to stop getting into hot water over his procrastination and to keep his job. His do-it-now solution was to attack procrastination and perfectionism at cognitive, emotional, and behavioral levels. As a by-product, he anticipated boosting his tolerance for his discomfort about the performance reviews.

Ted broke his complex procrastination habit into three challenges: (1) address his tendency to expect perfection from himself and make his worth depend on others' approval of his performances, (2) overcome his tendency to sidetrack himself when he felt uncomfortable about a timely task, and (3) behaviorally pursue the performance goals by refusing to divert himself.

- *Meeting the first challenge.* Ted seemed to enjoy resolving paradoxes. (1) He considered that John was okay even without 100 percent approval, so why should he treat himself differently? (2) He explored why he was able to accept that he could not turn 100 percent of his sales calls into sales, but he felt that he should please 100 percent of the sales staff with perfect performance reviews. Examining two potential contradictions showed a shift from a self-absorbed perfectionist view to a more self-observant one.

    Ted knew many reasons why you can't be 100 percent perfect in selling. A potential customer may have an established relationship with another sales representative and want to maintain it. A competitor may have a special pricing opportunity for the customer that he could not match. He may not have made a good personal connection because of style differences between himself and a purchasing agent. Sometimes he would never know the reason. Making this connection provided a way for Ted to generalize what he knew in one part of his life to a comparable area.

• *Meeting the second challenge.* Ted put himself into the position of looking over the materials for his performance reviews and allowing himself to feel the tension that would ordinarily start his procrastination process in motion. He allowed himself to live with the tension until his normal impulse to retreat vanished. This is the emotive way to cut through a procrastination barrier.

 Ted used two emotional tolerance-building techniques. (1) He looked for a connection between what he was thinking and what he was feeling. He told himself that he couldn't do it (meaning talking with the sales force about his ratings of them). He heard himself say, "I'll look like a fool." He observed that his level of discomfort jumped with those thoughts. He felt a strong urge to escape the tension. (2) Instead of retreating, Ted stuck with the tension. He also retrofitted his understanding of default procrastination self-statements. Just because they are automatic and linked to emotions, he discovered, doesn't make them true.

 Mapping the connection between his default negative thinking and his discomfort paid a dividend. He reported that this tension tolerance development exercise was the most important of the three. By accepting tension, he felt less tense.

- *Meeting the third challenge.* Ted understood that it was important for him to get past thinking and emotional barriers to boost his chances of permanently stopping procrastinating on the performance reviews. However, the third challenge involved putting his muscles in motion and writing the reviews. This *grinding it out phase* need not wait until meeting the first two challenges. He could do all three concomitantly.

  Ted's fear of going over the reviews with his salespeople was solved with practical new information. He rehearsed by starting with several positive comments followed by some developmental areas for improvement. Ted felt more comfortable with this structure. So, he applied it in practice.

By taking cognitive, emotive, and behavioral steps, Ted interrupted his procrastination process, redirected his thinking, and changed the outcome. Ted finished the reviews. He met with his staff. From his report, the reviews were generally well received.

Ted largely—but not completely—gave up on the idea that a single performance review had to be meaningful and perfect. Nevertheless, the next time performance reviews were due, Ted finished first.

Not all situations result in a relatively permanent and positive outcome. However, by targeting one tenacious procrastination situation, Ted learned techniques that he could apply to other such situations. Generalization, however, builds upon repeated application of what was learned in one situation to another to which the same process can be adapted or directly applied. Although opportunities to reapply what was learned may abound, application opportunities may not be clearly seen as separate examples of a similar procrastination process.

When the rider intentionally gains experience in applying counter-procrastination measures, the rider may have more to say about guiding the horse than the horse has to say about the rider's direction. The rider may often make the Y decision. But the horse never goes away. Lapses are expected. Still, regaining momentum is reasonable, provided that actions are taken. And the horse can also be fun. As the old saying goes, "All work and no play makes Jack a dull boy."

Resources

Introduction

Bandura, Albert. *Self-Efficacy: The Exercise of Control*. New York: Freeman, 1997.

Becket, S. *Waiting for Godot: Tragicomedy in 2 Acts*. New York: Grove Press, 1997.

Butler, A. C., J. E. Chapman, E. M. Forman, and A. T. Beck. "The Empirical Status of Cognitive-Behavioral Therapy: A Review of Meta-analyses." *Clinical Psychology Review* 26, no. 1 (2006): 17–31.

Ellis, A., and W. Knaus. *Overcoming Procrastination*. New York: New American Library, 1979.

Frost, R. "The Road Not Taken." *Mountain Interval*. New York: Henry Holt, 1916, p. 9.

Gilbert, D. *Stumbling on Happiness*. New York: Knopf, 2006.

Hayasji, J. "The Relationship Between Cognitive Content and Emotions Following Dilatory Behavior: Considering the Level of Trait Procrastination." *Japanese Journal of Psychology* 79(6) 2009: 514–521.

Henrich, J. B, R. Boyd, S. Bowles, et al. "'Economic Man' in Cross-Cultural Perspective: Behavioral Experiments in 15 Small-Scale Societies." *Behavioral and Brain Sciences* 28, no. 6 (2005): 795–855.

Klassen, R. M., L. L. Krawchuk, and S. Rajani. "Academic Procrastination of Undergraduates: Low Self-Efficacy to Self-Regulate Predicts Higher Levels of Procrastination." *Contemporary Educational Psychology* 33, no. 4 (2008): 915–931.

Knaus, W. "The Parameters of Procrastination." In *Cognition and Emotional Disorders*, R. Grieger and I. Grieger. New York: Human Sciences Press, 1981, pp 174-196.

Redding, R. E., J. D. Herbert, E. M. Forman, and B. A. Gaudiano. "Self-Help or Self-Hurt? Guidelines for Recommending Good Self-Help Books to Patients and the General Public." *Clinician's Research Digest* 27, no. 1 (2009); extracted from Redding, R. E., J. D. Herbert, E. M. Forman, and B. A. Gaudiano. "Popular Self-Help Books for Anxiety, Depression, and Trauma: How Scientifically Grounded and Useful Are They?" *Professional Psychology: Research and Practice* 39(5) (2008): 537–545.

Sirois, F. M. "'I'll Look After My Health Later': A Replication and Extension of the Procrastination Health Model with Community Dwelling Adults." *Personality and Individual Differences* 43, no. 1 (2007): 15–26.

Steel, P. "The Nature of Procrastination: A Meta-Analytic and Theoretical Review of Quintessential Self-Regulatory Failure." *Psychological Bulletin* 133, no. 1 (2007): 65–94.

Straus, J. N. *Stravinsky's Late Music*. Cambridge, U.K.: Cambridge University Press, 2004, p. 44.

Tice, D. M., and R. F. Baumeister. "Longitudinal Study of Procrastination, Performance, Stress, and Health: The Costs and Benefits of Dawdling." *Psychological Science* 8, no. 6 (1997): 454–458.

Chapter 1

Allport, G. *Personality: A Psychological Interpretation*. New York: Holt, Rinehart, & Winston, 1937.

Carpenter, R. H. S. "A Neural Mechanism That Randomizes Behavior." *Journal of Consciousness Studies* 6, no. 1 (1999): 13–22.

Darwin, C. *Expression of the Emotions in Man and Animals*. London: John Murray, Albemarle Street, 1872.

Korzybski, A. *Science and Sanity*. New York: The Science Press, 1933.

Liu, Z., B. J. Richmond,, E. A. Murray, R. C. Saunders, et al. "DNA Targeting of Rhinal Cortex D2 Receptor Protein Reversibly Blocks Learning of Cues That Predict Reward." *Proceedings of the National Academy of Sciences* 101, no. 33 (2004): 12336–12341.

Mazur, J. E. "Preference for Larger, More Delayed Work Requirements." *Journal of the Experimental Analysis of Behavior* 65, no. 1 (1996): 159–171.

———. "Procrastination by Pigeons with Fixed-Interval Response Requirements." *Journal of the Experimental Analysis of Behavior* 69, no. 2 (1998): 185–197.

McCrea, S. M., N. Liberman, Y. Trope, and S. J. Sherman. "Construal Level and Procrastination." *Psychological Science* 19, no. 12 (2008): 1308–1314.

Payot, J. *The Education of the Will*. New York: Funk & Wagnalls, 1909.

Chapter 2

David, D., A. Szentagotai, E. Kallay, and M. Bianca. "A Synopsis of Rational-Emotive Behavior Therapy: Fundamental and Applied Research." *Journal of Rational-Emotive and Cognitive-Behavior Therapy* 23 (2005): 175–221.

Ellis, A. *Ask Albert Ellis: Straight Answers and Sound Advice from America's Best-Known Psychologist*. Atascadero, Calif.: Impact Publishers, 2003.

Epictetus. *The Discourses of Epictetus: The Handbook, Fragments*. Translated by Robin Hard. Rutland, Vt.: Charles E, Tuddle, 1995

The Folly of Procrastination or the Story of Charles and Edward Martin. Philadelphia: American Sunday School Union, 1848.

Jones, E. E., and S. Berglas. "Control of Attributions about the Self through Self-Handicapping Strategies: The Appeal of Alcohol and the Role of Underachievement." *Personality and Social Psychology Bulletin* 4 (1978): 200–206.

Kazantzis, Nikolaos, Frank P. Deane, and Kevin R. Ronan. "Homework Assignments in Cognitive and Behavioral Therapy: A Meta-Analysis." *Clinical Psychology: Science and Practice* 7, no. 2 (2000): 189–202.

Medvec, V. H., S. F. Madey, and T. Gilovich. "When Less Is More: Counterfactual Thinking and Satisfaction among Olympic Medallists." *Journal of Personality and Social Psychology* 69 (1995): 603–610.

Sherman, S. J., and A. R. McConnell. "Dysfunctional Implications of Counterfactual Thinking: When Alternatives to Reality Fail Us." In

What Might Have Been: The Social Psychology of Counterfactual Thinking, edited by Neal J. Roese and James M. Olson, 199–231. Hillsdale, N.J.: Lawrence Erlbaum, 1995.

Sirois, F. M. "Procrastination and Counterfactual Thinking: Avoiding What Might Have Been." *British Journal of Social Psychology* 43 (2004): 269–286.

Wolitzky-Taylor, Kate B., Jonathan D. Horowitz, Mark B. Powers, and Michael J. Telch. "Psychological Approaches in the Treatment of Specific Phobias: A Meta-Analysis." *Clinical Psychology Review* 28, no. 6 (2008): 1021–1037.

Chapter 3

Baas, M., C. K. W. De Dreu, and B. A. Nijstad. "A Meta-analysis of 25 Years of Mood-Creativity Research: Hedonic Tone, Activation, or Regulatory Focus?" *Psychological Bulletin* 134, no. 6 (2008): 779–806.

Freud, S. *The Id and the Ego*. Translated by Joan Riviere. London: Hogarth Press, 1950.

Knaus, W. *The Cognitive Behavioral Workbook for Anxiety*. Oakland, Calif.: New Harbinger, 2008.

———. *How to Get Out of a Rut*. Englewood Cliffs, N.J.: Prentice-Hall, 1982.

von Clausewitz, C. *On War*. Edited by Anatol Rapoport. New York: Penguin, 1968.

Chapter 4

Aspinwall, L., and S. Taylor. "A Stitch in Time: Self-Regulation and Proactive Coping." *Psychological Bulletin* 121 (1998): 417–436.

Beswick, G., E. D. Rothblum, and L. Mann. "Psychological Antecedents of Student Procrastination." *Australian Psychologist* 23, no. 2 (1988): 207–217.

Binnewies, C., S. Sonnentag, and E. J. Mojza. "Feeling Recovered and Thinking about the Good Sides of One's Work." *Journal of Occupational Health Psychology* 14, no. 3 (2009): 243–256.

Blascovich, J. "Challenge and Threat." In *Handbook of Approach and*

Avoidance Motivation, edited by Andrew J. Elliot, 431–445. New York: Psychology Press, 2008.

Cheng, Grand H.-L., and Darius K.-S. Chan. "Who Suffers More from Job Insecurity? A Meta-Analytic Review." *Applied Psychology: An International Review* 57 (2008): 272–303.

Chida, Y., and A. Steptoe. "Cortisol Awakening Response and Psychosocial Factors: A Systematic Review and Meta-Analysis." *Biological Psychology* 80, no. 3 (2009): 265–278.

Flett, G. L., K. R. Blankstein, and T. R. Martin. "Procrastination, Negative Self-Evaluation, and Stress in Depression and Anxiety: A Review and Preliminary Model." In *Procrastination and Task Avoidance: Theory, Research, and Treatment*, edited by J. R. Ferrari, J. L. Johnson, and W. G. McCown, Plenum Series in Social/Clinical Psychology, 137–167. New York: Plenum Press, 1995.

Frankl, V. *Man's Search for Meaning*. Boston: Beacon, 2000.

Glei, D. A., N. Goldman, Y. Chaung, and M. Weinatein. "Do Chronic Stressors Lead to Physiological Disregulation? Testing the Theory of Allostatic Load." *Psychosomatic Medicine* 69 (2007): 769–776.

Greenglass, E. R., and L. Fiksenbaum. "Proactive Coping, Positive Affect, and Well-Being: Testing for Mediation Using Path Analysis." *European Psychologist* 14, no. 1 (2009): 29–39.

Halbesleben, Jonathon R. B., and Wm. Matthew Bowler. "Emotional Exhaustion and Job Performance: The Mediating Role of Motivation." *Journal of Applied Psychology* 92, no. 1 (2007): 93–106.

———, and M. Ronald Buckley. "Burnout in Organizational Life." *Journal of Management* 30, no. 6 (2004): 859–879.

Hammerfald, K., C. Eberle, M. Grau, et al. "Persistent Effects of Cognitive-Behavioral Stress Management on Cortisol Responses to Acute Stress in Healthy Subjects—A Randomized Controlled Trial." *Psychoneuroendocrinology* 31, no. 3 (2006): 333–339.

Jockers-Scherübl, M. C., D. Zubraegel, T. Baer, et al. "Nerve Growth Factor Serum Concentrations Rise after Successful Cognitive-Behavioural Therapy of Generalized Anxiety Disorder." *Progress in Neuro-Psychopharmacology & Biological Psychiatry* 31, no. 1 (2007): 200–204.

Knaus, W. *Change Your Life Now*. New York: John Wiley & Sons, 1994.

Maslach, C. "Burnout: A Multidimensional Perspective." In *Professional Burnout: Recent Developments in Research and Practice*, edited by

W. B. Schaufeli, C. Maslach, and T. Marek. Washington, D.C.: Taylor & Francis, 1993:19-32.

McEwen, B., & E. N. Lasley. "Allostatic Load: When Protection Gives Way to Damage." In Monat, Alan, Richard S. Lazarus, and Gretchen Reevy, eds. *The Praeger Handbook on Stress and Coping*, vol. 1, 99–109. Westport, Conn.: Praeger Publishers, 2007.

McEwen, B. S., and T. Seeman. "Stress and Affect: Applicability of the Concepts of Allostasis and Allostatic Load." In *Handbook of Affective Sciences*, edited by R. J. Davidson, K. R. Scherer, and H. H. Goldsmith, 1117–1137. New York: Oxford University Press, 2003.

Miller, G. E., E. Chen, and E. S. Zhou. "If It Goes Up, Must It Come Down? Chronic Stress and the Hypothalamic-Pituitary-Adrenocortical Axis in Humans." *Psychological Bulletin* 133, no. 1 (2007): 25–45.

Myrtek, M. "Type A Behavior and Hostility as Independent Risk Factors for Coronary Heart Disease." In *Contributions toward Evidence-Based Psychocardiology: A Systematic Review of the Literature*, edited by Jochen Jordan, Benjamin Bardé, and Andreas Michael Zeiher, 159–183. Washington, D.C.: American Psychological Association, 2007.

NIOSH. "Stress at Work." U.S. National Institute for Occupational Safety and Health, DHHS Publication 99-101, 1999.

Phillips, K. M., M. H. Antoni, S. C. Lechner, et al. "Stress Management Intervention Reduces Serum Cortisol and Increases Relaxation during Treatment for Nonmetastatic Breast Cancer." *Psychosomatic Medicine* 70, no. 9 (2008): 1044–1049.

Range, F., L. Horn, Z. Viranyi, and L. Huber. "The Absence of Reward Induces Inequity Aversion in Dogs." *Proceedings of the National Academy of Sciences* 106, no. 1 (2009): 340–345.

Roberts, A. D. L., A. S. Papadopoulos, S. Wessely, et al. "Salivary Cortisol Output Before and After Cognitive Behavioural Therapy for Chronic Fatigue Syndrome." *Journal of Affective Disorders* 115, no. 1–2 (2009): 280–286.

Shea, T. "For Many Employees, the Workplace Is Not a Satisfying Place." *HR Magazine* 28 (2002): 47.

Sohl, S. J., and A. Moyer. "Refining the Conceptualization of a Future-Oriented Self-Regulatory Behavior: Proactive Coping." *Personality and Individual Differences* 47, no. 2 (2009): 139–144.

Stöber, J., and J. Joormann. "Worry, Procrastination, and Perfectionism: Differentiating Amount of Worry, Pathological Worry, Anxiety, and Depression." *Cognitive Therapy and Research* 25, no. 1 (2001): 49–60.

Sverke, Magnus, Johnny Hellgren, and Katharina Näswall. "No Security: A Meta-Analysis and Review of Job Insecurity and Its Consequences." *Journal of Occupational Health Psychology* 7 (2002): 242–264.

van Wolkenten, M., S. F. Brosnan, and F. B. M. de Waal. "Inequity Responses of Monkeys Modified by Effort." *Proceedings of the National Academy of Sciences* 104, no. 47 (2007): 18854–18859.

Yerkes, R. M., and J. D. Dodson. "The Relation of Strength of Stimulus to Rapidity of Habit-Formation." *Journal of Comparative Neurology and Psychology* 18 (1908): 459–482.

Chapter 5

Chiri, L. R., and C. Sica. "Psychological, Physiological and Psychopathological Aspects of the Construct of 'Worry.'" *Giornale Italiano di Psicologia* 34, no 3 (2007): 531–552.

Gilbert, D. T., and P. S. Malone. "The Correspondence Bias." *Psychological Bulletin* 117, no. 1 (1995): 21–38.

Kahneman, D. "A Perspective on Judgment and Choice: Mapping Bounded Rationality." *American Psychologist* 58, no. 9 (2003): 697–720.

Knaus, W. *The Cognitive Behavioral Workbook for Anxiety.* Oakland, Calif.: New Harbinger, 2008.

———, and C. Hendricks. *The Illusion Trap.* New York: World Almanac, 1986.

Spada, M. M., K. Hiou, and A. V. Nikcevic. "Metacognitions, Emotions, and Procrastination." *Journal of Cognitive Psychotherapy* 20, no. 3 (2006): 319–326.

Sun Tzu. *The Art of War.* Lionel Giles, trans. New York: Barnes & Noble Classics, 2003.

Tversky, A., and D. Kahneman. "The Framing of Decisions and the Psychology of Choice." *Science* 211, no. 4481 (1981): 453–458.

von Clausewitz, C. *On War.* New York: Penguin, 1968.

Chapter 6

Aesop. *Aesop's Fables.* Translated by V.S. Vernon Jones. New York: Avenel Books, 1912.

Birdi, K., C. Clegg, M. Patterson, et al. "The Impact of Human Resource and Operational Management Practices on Company Productivity: A Longitudinal Study." *Personnel Psychology* 61, no. 3 (2008): 467–501.

Butler, D. L., and P. H. Winne. "Feedback and Self-Regulated Learning: A Theoretical Synthesis." *Review of Educational Research* 65 (1995): 245–281.

Gallagher, R. P., A. Golin, and K. Kelleher. "The Personal, Career, and Learning Skills Needs of College Students." *Journal of College Student Development* 33, no. 4 (1992): 301–309.

Gordy, J. P. *Lessons in Psychology, Designed Especially for Private Students, and as a Textbook in Secondary Schools.* Columbus, Ohio: Hann & Adair Printers, 1890.

Jones, S. "Instructions, Self-Instructions and Performance." *Quarterly Journal of Experimental Psychology* 20, no. 1 (1968): 74–78.

Kozlowski, S. W. J., and R. P. DeShon. "Enhancing Learning Performance and Adaptability for Complex Tasks." Final Report: U.S. Grant No. F49620-01-1-0283, 2005.

Lonergan, J. M., and K. J. Maher. "The Relationship between Job Characteristics and Workplace Procrastination as Moderated by Locus of Control." *Journal of Social Behavior & Personality* 15 (2000): 213–224.

Malouff, J. M., and C. Murphy. "Effects of Self-Instructions on Sport Performance." *Journal of Sport Behavior* 29, no. 2 (2006): 159–168.

Meichenbaum, D., and J. Goodman. "Training Impulsive Children to Talk to Themselves." *Journal of Abnormal Psychology* 77, no. 2 (1971): 115–126.

Pintrich, P. R., and E. V. De Groot. "Motivational and Self-Regulated Learning Components of Classroom Academic Performance." *Journal of Educational Psychology* 82, no. 1 (1990): 33–40.

Premack, D. "Reinforcement Theory." In *Nebraska Symposium on Motivation*, edited by D. Levine. Lincoln: University of Nebraska Press, 1965.

Shell, D. F., and J. Husman. "Control, Motivation, Affect, and Strategic Self-Regulation in the College Classroom: A Multidimensional

Phenomenon." *Journal of Educational Psychology* 100, no. 2 (2008): 443–459.

Vrugt, A., and F. J. Oort. "Metacognition, Achievement Goals, Study Strategies and Academic Achievement: Pathways to Achievement." *Metacognition and Learning* 3, no. 2 (2008): 123–146.

Wolitzky-Taylor, K. B., J. D. Horowitz, M. B. Powers, and M. J. Telch. "Psychological Approaches in the Treatment of Specific Phobias: A Meta-Analysis." *Clinical Psychology Review* 28, no. 6 (2008): 1021–1037.

Chapter 7

Ainslie, G. "Précis of Breakdown of Will." *Behavioral and Brain Sciences* 28, no. 5 (2005): 635–673.

———. "Specious Reward: A Behavioral Theory of Impulsiveness and Impulse Control." *Psychological Bulletin* 82, no. 4 (1975): 463–496.

Birdi, K., C. Clegg, M. Patterson, et al. "The Impact of Human Resource and Operational Management Practices on Company Productivity: A Longitudinal Study." *Personnel Psychology* 61, no. 3 (2008): 467–501.

Bowling, N. A. "Is the Job Satisfaction-Job Performance Relationship Spurious? A Meta-Analytic Examination." *Journal of Vocational Behavior* 71 (2007): 167–185.

Fiske, S. T., and S. E. Taylor. *Social Cognition*, 2nd ed. New York: McGraw-Hill, 1991.

Hochwarter, Wayne A., Mary Dana Laird, and Robyn L. Brouer. "Board Up the Windows: The Interactive Effects of Hurricane-Induced Job Stress and Perceived Resources on Work Outcomes." *Journal of Management* 34 (2008): 263–289.

Höcker, A., M. Engberding, J. Beissner, and F. Rist. "Working Steps Aiming at Punctuality and Realistic Planning." *Verhaltenstherapie* 19, no. 1 (2009): 28–32.

Holland, J. L. "Exploring Careers with a Typology: What We Have Learned and Some New Directions." *American Psychologist* 51 (1996): 397–406.

Howell, A. J., and K. Buro. "Implicit Beliefs, Achievement Goals, and Procrastination: A Mediational Analysis." *Learning and Individual Differences* 19, no. 1 (2009): 151–154.

Judge, T. A., C. J. Thoresen, J. E. Bono, and G. K. Patton. "The Job Satisfaction-Job Performance Relationship: A Qualitative and Quantitative Review." *Psychological Bulletin* 127 (2001): 376–407.

Knaus, W. J. "A Cognitive Perspective on Organizational Change." *Journal of Cognitive Therapy* 6, no. 4 (1992): 278–284.

—————. *Take Charge Now: Powerful Techniques for Breaking the Blame Game.* New York: John Wiley & Sons, 2000.

Lonergan, J. M., and K. J. Maher. "The Relationship between Job Characteristics and Workplace Procrastination as Moderated by Locus of Control." *Journal of Social Behavior & Personality* 15 (2000): 213–224.

Ng, T. W. H., K. L. Sorensen, and L. T. Eby. "Locus of Control at Work: A Meta-Analysis." *Journal of Organizational Behavior* 27 (2006): 1057–1087.

O'Donoghue, T., and M. Rabin. "Choice and Procrastination." Institute of Business and Economic Research, Department of Economics, University of California, Berkeley, Paper E00'281, 2000.

Schurz, Carl. Speech. Boston, April 18, 1859.

Tracey, T. J. G., and S. B. Robbins. "The Interest-Major Congruence and College Success Relation: A Longitudinal Study." *Journal of Vocational Behavior* 69 (2006): 64–89.

Tsabari, O., A. Tziner, and E. I. Meir. "Updated Meta-analysis on the Relationship between Congruence and Satisfaction." *Journal of Career Assessment* 13 (2005): 216–232.

Index

About the Author

William Knaus, Ed.D., is a licensed clinical psychologist and former psychology professor. As a renowned authority, he has authored over 20 books on anxiety, depression and mental health, and procrastination. He is a pioneer in cognitive revolution in psychotherapy and one of the original directors of postdoctoral training in rational emotive behavioral therapy. He conducted seminars for PESI, a national organization that sponsors continuing education for mental health and medical professionals. Aside from his private practice, Knaus was a consultant for numerous organizations, such as the U.S. Army and the Strathmore Paper Company.

CPSIA information can be obtained at www.ICGtesting.com
Printed in the USA
BVOW011739280413

319266BV00007B/19/P